Wake-Up Call

Economic, Political, Social, and Psychological Factors That Can Erode Your Wealth

TIM CHANG

iUniverse, Inc.
Bloomington

Wake-Up Call
Economic, Political, Social, and Psychological
Factors That Can Erode Your Wealth

iUniverse books may be ordered through booksellers or by contacting:

iUniverse
1663 Liberty Drive
Bloomington, IN 47403
www.iuniverse.com
1-800-Authors (1-800-288-4677)

Cover design: LSDdesign

Discover other titles by Tim Chang at Smashwords.com. Visit Tim Chang's blog at www.manage-financial-wealth.com for more helpful tips on protecting and growing your wealth.

ISBN: 978-1-4759-8915-1 (sc)
ISBN: 978-1-4759-8916-8 (e)

Library of Congress Control Number: 2013908151

Printed in the United States of America

iUniverse rev. date: 06/03/2013

Wake-Up Call:

Economic, Political, Social, and Psychological
Factors That Can Erode Your Wealth

CONTENTS

ACKNOWLEDGEMENTS

THIS BOOK WOULD not have been possible without the support and encouragement of my wife Jane and my four children Lake, Ahbi, Szewei, and Weiyi. I would also like to extend my gratitude to Cynthia Rurak and Jared McGeough for helping me to shape my ideas into words, and for their useful advice during the book's many stages on how to best bring these ideas to light. I would further like to express my thanks to those clients who, over the years, have helped me become more aware of the typical mistakes that nearly everyone makes on the way to achieving their financial goals. Finally, I wish to acknowledge the many professionals, small business owners, and entrepreneurs striving to protect their assets and succeed on their own terms in today's economy. Your experiences inspired me to write this book and to use my professional knowledge to show how, with the right advice, it is possible to succeed financially even in difficult times.

INTRODUCTION

"If you want to make your dreams come true, the first thing you have to do is wake up." – J. M. Powe

IN THE 1988 science-fiction thriller *They Live* directed by John Carpenter, a drifter by the name of Nada travels to Los Angeles hoping to find a job. Soon after arriving, he steps into a church that had mysteriously been raided by the police the night before. Once inside, he happens upon a box full of what appears to be normal, everyday sunglasses. Taking a pair for himself, Nada leaves the church and walks down Los Angeles' fashionable Rodeo Drive, where he tries on his new glasses for the first time. Nada discovers that rather than merely shield his eyes from the sun, the glasses completely change his perception of the world, revealing the subliminal messages used in everyday advertising by the political and financial elite to hypnotize ordinary people into compliance and consumerism.

Everywhere Nada looks while wearing the glasses appears different: a billboard for a computer company now displays one simple word, "Obey"; a sign advertising an expensive men's clothing store ("Armisi's Men's Apparel") now reads "No Independent Thought"; and the sign in a window that normally reads "Sale" has become "Consume." Up and down the busy street, signs, billboards, book and magazine covers, are all transformed through the strange glasses: "Stay Asleep," "Buy," "Do Not Question." Later in the film, another character explains that the glasses exist because "the world needs a wake-up call." The population needs

1

to start seeing things as they really are, to cut through the distorted messages handed down by the media and the politicians about who people really are, what their money can do for them, and what's best for their future.

Although over twenty years old, much of Carpenter's film still resonates today. At the beginning of the film, for example, Nada tells an employment officer that he's just lost a job he held for ten years in Colorado: "things just seemed to dry up," Nada says, "they lost fourteen banks in one week." One of the construction workers Nada meets talks about how he lost his job when the steel mills in Detroit finally went under. All of this should sound familiar, especially after the highly publicized near collapse of big American investment banks like Lehmann Brothers during the subprime mortgage crisis of the late 2000s, the high unemployment rates that followed the financial crisis of 2008, and the catastrophic failure of the automotive industry between 2008 and 2010.

Yet, as tempting as it might be to blame the financial crises and subsequent economic recession on those big companies that abused the free market system, we can't shirk our own responsibility. As billionaire investor Warren Buffet once wrote, "all hard work leads to profit; but mere talk leads only to poverty."[1] In today's economy, those educated, ambitious, and skilled enough to have either started their own businesses or managed to succeed in professional positions are still at risk financially. More often than not, it's because they fail to monitor the potential impact of national and international political and economic events on the financial market or to recognize how their own sometimes illogical, emotion-driven thinking can lead to investment mistakes. In this respect, we should revise Buffett's remark for our contemporary moment: "all *smart* work leads to profit, but merely *blind* work leads only to failure."

Therefore, just like the sunglasses in Carpenter's film, this book provides a clarifying vision of the world as it really is, not as we're told it is, so that we can achieve a secure financial future for ourselves and our loved ones. While most of us aren't in any kind of a position to affect how big banks, governments, and corporations do business, we are capable of educating ourselves about those issues that can and do affect our financial security. We must become aware of the current economic crises and the role they have on our own financial well-being. By taking an honest look at the political, social, geographic, psychological, and cultural contexts and factors affecting our finances in today's globalized economy, we can begin to understand the external factors affecting our economic environment, and reflect on our own decision errors, fears, and biases. Although the challenges facing the self-employed professional, creative entrepreneur, or independent business owner can seem daunting, I believe that those who educate themselves about financial matters, question received wisdom about investing, and take responsibility for their financial well-being, can better protect their money, their business, and their financial legacy.

Economically speaking, in most Western countries there are essentially three classes of people. We traditionally think of class in terms of upper, middle, and lower, but it would be more accurate to say that classes are divided into 1) a political and bureaucratic public-sector class with overly generous benefits plans; 2) business owners, entrepreneurs, and self-employed professionals whose ingenuity and industry create wealth; and 3) everyone else who often unfairly bear the heaviest tax burden,. The last thing we should do is trust the political class to guide us to economic safety. Along with celebrity culture, the political class specializes in misrepresentation and manipulation to keep the general public "asleep." Let's take a recent example: the November 2012 re-election of President Barack Obama in the United States (US). One day after the election, media in the US already began talking about how the nation was headed towards a fiscal cliff. After five years of economic recession both in the US and around the world, 2013 will see massive cuts in US government spending and, perhaps most significantly, expiration of the tax cuts implemented by former president George W. Bush. With the expiration of the Bush tax cuts, Obama now has a better opportunity to do what he's been saying he would do for the last four years: dramatically increase taxes on the wealthiest US citizens.

But taxing the rich isn't viable economic policy. As I go on to explore in more detail in Chapter Four, history shows that higher taxes for the rich doesn't actually generate higher revenue or encourage economic growth; in fact, it's just the opposite. At best, "tax the rich" offers a good sound bite that panders to the middle-class and the left-leaning base of Democratic voters. This kind of socialist-lite rhetoric might sound nice, but it poses serious problems for economic recovery. And if recovery is the ultimate goal, higher taxes on the wealthy and big business can actually be counterproductive. Although the US government criticized manufacturers for moving operations offshore, by making them pay higher taxes, they're unwittingly driving manufacturing companies away to seek tax breaks and cheaper labor elsewhere. During his first term, Obama rightly came down hard on greedy investment bankers whose desire for short-term profit sparked the subprime mortgage crisis in 2008. But the regulatory strictures that the US government put in place also "failed to differentiate between Wall Street's culprits and the great majority of American businesses." These undeserved reprimands "unleashed a regulatory witch-hunt" that forced corporations to spend money on "costly, unproductive legal defences" rather than focus on job creation.[2] The result: very little growth, more deficit spending, and a 60% hike in national debt over the last four years.[3]

Yet it was Obama's opponent, Republican Mitt Romney, who was roundly criticized for commenting that the 47% of Americans who support Obama don't earn enough to pay income taxes.[4] Many on the left and in the media perceived Romney's comment as callous and alienating. To be sure, Romney's comment wasn't good electoral politics and it was even slightly misleading, since about two-thirds of the 47% actually do pay some form of state income, payroll, and sales tax.[5] Nonetheless, Romney's comment *did* shed light on a serious problem: far too many people have become dependent on government social programs, and the strain on public coffers is reaching a breaking point. Given Romney's past experience in the private sector, his remarks should have spurred the Obama administration to think harder about encouraging job and wealth creation; instead, the broader American public chose to believe the easy narrative: that the wealthy, *the very people that drive economic growth*, are at the root of America's problems. Even Canadian politicians are jumping at the chance to scapegoat the wealthy, with high-profile personalities like Justin Trudeau suggesting that "virtually all of the benefit of [Canada's economic] growth has accrued to a small number of wealthy Canadians."[6] Instead of encouraging people to take personal responsibility for their finances by educating themselves and improving their skills to meet the demands of the job market, politicians are basically telling them: "hey, don't worry, you're not to blame. It's the fault of the rich! You don't have to change a thing."

This type of rhetoric is entirely misleading. Our economic problems are not caused by the "1%." The idea that only a small group of rich elites enjoy the benefits of economic growth in the US or Canada is a myth, a placebo, a sugar pill meant to keep the majority of people asleep. In Canada, a 2011 study by the Simon Fraser Institute demonstrated that the poorest Canadians, and not the rich, are the ones experiencing the most significant increases in income over the last two decades. From 1990 to 2009, the average income of individuals in the bottom 20% of Canadian earners increased from $6,000 to just over $38,000 per year. Astonishingly, the study further showed that two out of every five Canadians in the bottom 20% in 1990 had risen into the top 40% of income earners by 2009.[7] Income inequality is not nearly as pronounced as the political class insists. The top 20% of income earners over the same ten-year period increased only 23%, which pales in comparison to the 635% jump in average income for the lowest 20%.[8] The rich *aren't* getting richer and the poor *aren't* getting poorer: the poor, in fact, are getting richer.

What these numbers suggest is that the so-called super-rich haven't been hoarding wealth so much as creating a significant amount of income growth for those unable to take the risk of diving into the business world. Despite this fact, we continue to see union bosses claim that the very people supplying their members with jobs are the bad guys. To take a recent example, the heads of the Bakery, Confectionery, Tobacco Workers & Grain Millers International Union somehow convinced employees at US baking company Hostess to take job action, even though the company had filed for bankruptcy protection. Although the company they worked for was going under, the union refused to grant any concessions for a new collective bargaining agreement that would have allowed Hostess to keep its doors open. Instead, the union's job action resulted in the closure of three US plants and the layoff of over 600 workers. Chief Executive Gregory Rayburn also noted that the company's dire financial straits meant that it "didn't have much more wiggle room in terms of shutting down additional plants and that the next step would probably be a complete shutdown" or "possible liquidation."[9]

But rather than encourage their members to make lifestyle changes, or make shared sacrifices with the administration in order to keep their jobs, the union made a decision that will put their members' livelihoods at stake. *This* is protecting workers? Do the workers themselves realize that their noble union bosses sacrifice *nothing* if Hostess goes under, since they'll still have other unions to exploit elsewhere? Blindly following leaders all too willing to sell them out, the workers themselves end up without jobs, just another statistic in the devastating unemployment numbers ravaging the North American economy. In this respect, the prognosis doesn't look good for unions. As I go on to discuss in Chapter Two, the Hostess situation is just one of several highly publicized rows in recent years that has turned public opinion against unions.[10] As public-sector unions begin to renegotiate new contracts in the coming years, they will be forced to make further concessions on their benefits and pensions, which in many cases have become far too expensive for the economy to support.

In today's economy, our most valuable resource isn't something like labor or even oil, but entrepreneurial ingenuity and capital. By overtaxing the rich, the US stands to lose considerable amounts of both. Take billionaire co-founder of Facebook Eduardo Saverin, for instance. In the face of rising taxes on capital gains and dividends, Saverin decided to renounce his US citizenship, move to Singapore, and invest more heavily in Asian markets. Renouncing citizenship is an option chosen by increasing numbers of Americans. According to *Bloomberg*, a "record 1,780 gave up their US passports last year compared with 235 in 2008."[11] And with tax rates going up, that number is likely to get even higher. The tax-the-rich policy has given rise to an economic brain drain in the US: the best educated and most innovative businesspeople simply choose to grow their wealth elsewhere.

Canada isn't immune from these kinds of problems either. Because of its already-high income tax rates, Canada suffers a competitive disadvantage in attracting and maintaining skilled workers and entrepreneurs. At 45%, Canada boasts one of the highest combined federal-provincial income tax rates among the G-7 countries. In 2012, that combined rate "was higher than the comparable rate in every U.S. state except three."[12] This has created Canada's own brain-drain, especially with respect to young, highly-skilled post-graduates in fields such as computer science and engineering. As early as 2000, economics researchers David Zarifa and David Walters had already discovered a significant earnings gap between skilled graduates who stayed in Canada and those who moved to the US. In skilled professions such as computer science and engineering, those who relocated to the US were found to have significantly higher annual earnings.[13] As Canadian billionaire investor Seymour Schulich puts it, "'if you get too crazy [with taxing high-income earners]—I'm not going to move at my age . . . but the younger guys can move. You're going to lose a lot of good people. You get what happened in Europe. You get all your rich people who are migrating'."[14] This should be seen as a disaster. And yet the political class would have the majority believe that we should punish those intelligent and hard-working enough to succeed by redistributing their wealth? I'm not buying it, and neither should you.

A far greater problem than the super-rich is a general public misled by easy-to-swallow sound bites from the political class that obscure economic realities. It seems that whoever can better mislead the majority about taxing the rich will inevitably find themselves back in power, ready and willing to make the same mistakes over again to appease the public. But history has proven that socialist-style tax-and-spend policies don't work and never will. A core value of the capitalist economy in which we live is competition: competition drives innovation and development. Those best able to adapt to, and thus compete, within current economic conditions are those best equipped to survive.

But in the political arena, the fittest survivors seem to be those best able to manipulate public opinion. And the public appears all too willing to blindly accept the narratives that politicians dole out. When Romney spoke of the 47%, he spoke of a public whose dependency on government had also given them a sense of entitlement, a public who see themselves as victims rather than complicit in their own economic misfortunes. In the face of public approval, politicians start to believe in their own words, fancying themselves experts when it comes to the free market. But this is simply not the case: politicians shouldn't assume that because they can win an election, they can effectively plan an economy. Governments should not, and must not, be allowed to pick winners and losers when it comes to the economy. The government's role should be limited to constructing regulative frameworks that protect the public from the bad behavior of corporations and big banks. Clear, but limited, government regulations must be created that best serve the interests of the free market, rather than bog it down with inefficiencies, bureaucratic red tape, or ideological agendas sanctioned by an under-educated public.

The chapters that follow tackle many of these issues, and much more. This book will give you a clearer view of the economic world picture, and call attention to the kinds of common mistakes, biases, and cultural factors that affect financial decision-making and how these factors work in our everyday behavior. The book organizes the various factors affecting personal wealth into two parts: "Macroeconomic Factors" and "Microeconomic Factors." Macroeconomics studies those factors that affect the economy as a whole, focusing on economic decisions made by large social and political forces, such as governments and nations. Microeconomics, on the other hand, deals with the "small," those aspects or factors that influence the economic decisions made at the level of the individual. To put it simply, macroeconomics takes a top-down approach, from the whole to its constituent parts, while microeconomics works from the bottom up, from the part to the whole. Although these two areas study quite different phenomena, they in fact complement one another. By addressing both macro and microeconomic factors, this book encourages you to think of these factors as interdependent, as having an equal influence on your financial wealth.

Our exploration of macroeconomic factors begins in Part One by posing the question of how decisions by North American governments got us into this economic mess in the first place. You may have heard about the US housing crisis in connection to the broader global recession; this first chapter explores this connection, focusing on how the US housing bubble and the crisis that followed set the stage for the economic problems facing us today. The US housing crisis is important not only because it serves as the main catalyst for the broader economic recession, but also for giving us a glimpse into how poor government policy, the misbehavior of the big banks, and psychological factors such as fear and greed generated a global crisis.

Part One continues with a look at the pros and cons of another major macroeconomic factor, globalization. Globalization describes the main phenomenon in which all economic activities take place today. The chapter provides a working definition of globalization, explores the drawbacks and benefits of a globalized economy, the European debt crisis, labor relations, and some ideas as to how global finance can be better coordinated to create better, fairer, economic practices.

Chapter Three tackles recent debates about the end of geography, that is, debates over whether physical geography still matters in our globally integrated economy. After introducing the concept of economic geography and the arguments for and against the end of geography, I look at a few examples of countries with beneficial and not-so-beneficial economic geographies, including Canada, Africa, and the Middle East. This chapter also addresses the economic costs of environmentalism and the recent controversy over the Keystone XL pipeline.

In Chapter Four, I take a critical view of current government approaches to regulation, bailouts, stimulus and austerity approaches to deficit reduction, government tax and social policy, and how bureaucracy and corruption conspire to thwart economic growth. The final chapter of Part One looks at how big commercial and investment banks abuse the trust placed in them by the public. Excessive deregulation, lack of transparency, legal and political loopholes, dishonest bookkeeping, and credit card debt, are just some of the ways that many big banks profit from customers like you. By shining a light on these practices, you will understand the ways in which banks often mistreat the public they are supposed to serve, and hopefully lead you to reflect more carefully on your own dealings with these institutions.

Where Part One emphasizes macroeconomic factors beyond our immediate control, Part Two focuses on microeconomic factors that affect the economic decisions made by individuals. If Part One "zooms out" to give you a view of the big issues that affect the economy as a whole, Part Two "zooms in" to focus on your own decision-making processes and clarifies the obstacles to working smarter when it comes to personal finance. Part Two thus provides you with some insight into how complex it can be to manage your own finances, and seeks to make you more aware of your own behavior.

In Chapter Six, I look at some of the most common personality types—the procrastinator, the know-it-all, the nervous Nellie, the people pleaser, and the dreamer—and how they influence the way people make decisions with their money. I then outline an ideal personality type towards which you can aspire: the disciplined investor. By analyzing the effects of personality-driven biases, this chapter provides you with insight into how to control and limit bad financial decisions and achieve the goal of becoming a disciplined investor.

In Chapter Seven, I shift from personality biases to cultural ones, or biases encoded within the shared set of values, beliefs, and assumptions that a certain group or society passes down from one generation to the next. However independent we think we are, our ethnicity, gender, religion, family relationships, the media, and nationality play a significant role in our day-to-day choices when it comes to money. Hence, Chapter Seven looks at the conscious and unconscious workings of culture on our financial decisions, while providing a critique of the way in which the media transmits a culture of consumerism that steadily erodes traditional values based on thrift, honesty, a strong work ethic, and a sense of personal responsibility.

The focus on financial decision-making continues in Chapter Eight, which addresses how the brain actually works when it comes to making decisions related to money. Looking at current research in behavioral finance, I explore some of our most common built-in biases, including our tendencies toward self-deception, confirmation of our beliefs, reacting with fear and greed and how these emotions fuel economic crises, and what behavioral economists call "hyperbolic discounting," or the tendency for someone to prefer a reward that arrives sooner rather than later.

These chapters lay the groundwork for the penultimate chapter, which provides you with a financial manifesto, a few simple guidelines on how to create and maintain an investment plan that's right for you. After outlining this financial manifesto, my concluding chapter offers some advice on how to choose a financial planner that's right for you, your business, and your family.

Both Parts One and Two offer analyses, gained throughout my thirty years of experience in financial services, of the world-economic situation and how to avoid some of the most common mistakes that people make when it comes to managing their money. The purpose of this book is primarily to educate and to challenge commonplace assumptions by providing an honest, independent analysis of the economic, political, social, and personal factors that can inhibit your ability to protect your assets and grow your wealth. Above all, however, this book encourages you to think for yourself, and to refuse the herd mentality that, like the signs in *They Live*, secretly enjoin us to "Obey" and go about business as usual. Ironically, I believe that the best way to begin thinking for yourself is to know your own limitations. The Greek philosopher Socrates famously remarked that the beginning of all wisdom is ignorance, knowing that you don't know enough. It is my sincere hope that this book guides you down the path of financial wisdom and encourages you to seek the advice of a certified financial planner to help secure your financial well-being. It's time to wake up.

ENDNOTES

[1] Warren Buffet qtd. in "Recession Survival Tips," African Bank, N.d. <https://www.africanbank.co.za/StaticAbilWeb/customer_education/money_management_recession_survival_tips.html>

[2] Gwyn Morgan, "Four More Years of Demonizing American Big Business," *Globe and Mail*, 18 November 2012. <http://www.theglobeandmail.com/report-on-business/four-more-years-of-demonizing-american-big-business/article5406563/?cmpid=rss1>

[3] Ibid.

[4] David Corn, "Secret Video: Romney Tells Millionaire Donors What He REALLY Thinks of Obama Supporters," *Mother Jones*, 17 September 2012. <http://www.motherjones.com/politics/2012/09/secret-video-romney-private-fundraiser>

[5] Jeremy Hobson, "The Numbers Behind Mitt Romney's 47% Comment," 18 September 2012. <http://www.marketplace.org/topics/elections/campaign-trail/numbers-behind-mitt-romneys-47-comment>

[6] Justin Trudeau, "Canadian Middle-Class Left Out of the Growth Equation," *Toronto Star*, 30 October 2012. <http://www.thestar.com/opinion/editorialopinion/article/1280029--canadian-middle-class-left-out-of-the-growth-equation>

[7] Niels Velthuis and Charles Lammam, "'Poor' Getting Richer." *Financial Post*, 20 November 2012. <http://opinion.financialpost.com/2012/11/20/poor-getting-richer/>

[8] Ibid.

[9] Rachel Feintzeig, "Hostess Closes Plants as Workers Strike," *Wall Street Journal*, 12 November 2012. <http://online.wsj.com/article/SB10001424127887324439804578114862262799942.html>

[10] Danny King, "Public Opinon of Unions Remains Near Quareter-Century Low," *Daily Finance*, 17 February 2011. <http://www.dailyfinance.com/2011/02/17/public-opinion-of-unions-remains-near-quarter-century-low/>

[11] Danielle Kucera, Sanat Vallikappan, and Christine Harper, "Facebook Co-Founder Saverin Gives Up US Citizenship Before IPO," *Bloomberg*, 11 May 2012. <http://www.bloomberg.com/news/2012-05-11/facebook-co-founder-saverin-gives-up-u-s-citizenship-before-ipo.html>

[12] Charles Lammam and Jason Clemens, "Don't Tax the Rich," *Huffington Post*, January 2013. <http://www.huffingtonpost.ca/charles-lammam/taxes-high-earners_b_2535524.html>

[13] David Zarifa and David Walters, "Revisiting Canada's Brain Drain: Evidence from the 2000 Cohort of Canadian University Graduates," *Canadian Public Policy*, Vol. 34, No. 3 (2008).

[14] Seymour Schulich qtd. in "Should Canadian Millionaires Pay More Taxes?" by Mark Gollem, CBC News, 20 December 2011. <http://www.cbc.ca/news/business/story/2011/12/09/canadian-millionaires-taxes.html>

PART ONE

Macroeconomic Factors

Chapter One

GOOD INTENTIONS, BAD DECISIONS: THE US HOUSING CRISIS

*"Housing bubble? What housing bubble? The signs are in place
for a further run-up in real estate. Breathe easy, mortgage holders.
There's still no place like home." – Jim Kramer, December 2003*

*"The stability . . . in US housing was likely a false calm before
a bigger storm. There are millions of homeowners under
threat of losing their homes." – Derek Holt, November 2009*

WHERE TO BEGIN when discussing the how's and whys of the
global economic recession? For most economists and analysts, the best
answer is the US housing bubble and the crisis that followed when the
bubble finally burst. The housing crisis itself was a combination of bad
government policy, overconfidence, lack of transparency, greed, fear, and
unnecessary risk, the seeds from which grew the global financial crisis.
In this respect, these issues also provide something of a microcosm of
the issues that I will take up in the chapters that make up the rest of Part
One. For now, this chapter will consider some of the major causes that
led to the housing bubble, including former president George W. Bush's
emphasis on the US as an ownership society, the use of government-
sponsored enterprises (GSEs), the ensuing subprime mortgage crisis, and
the global effects of this crisis.

Though the financial crisis of recent years is a complex phenomenon, the US housing crisis certainly played a major part in hastening problems that would lead to the broader recession; for all intents and purposes, the housing market was the first domino to fall. By grasping this fact, you will hopefully become more aware of how the housing crisis led to the current recession, as well as begin to become more aware of the kinds of economic practices and attitudes that lead governments, banks, and individuals to make serious financial blunders. With some understanding of the context in which such errors took place, you will have a better sense of how to confront the challenges that come with investing in today's markets.

"Housing Bubble? What Housing Bubble?"

One of the best known formulas for understanding periods of financial crisis is the law of boom and bust. Boom and bust explains how financial crises are brought about by monetary excess in periods of growth, which eventually lead to a contraction or slowing of economic growth and production in the following bust period. The US housing bubble demonstrates what happens when governments choose to ignore this law and instead concentrate on political ambitions, albeit combined with good intentions, and kowtow to the business interests of their campaign donors.

One of the main causes of the US housing bubble was that the Federal Reserve and former president Bush didn't heed the risks involved in playing with the law of boom and bust. As Jo Becker, Sheryl Gay Stolberg, and Stephen Labaton point out in a 2008 article for the *New York Times*, eight years after vowing to "spread the dream of homeownership," President Bush left the White House "'faced with the prospect of a global melt down' with roots in the housing sector he so ardently championed." Although a number of factors led to the current housing crisis, from "lenders who peddled easy credit, [to] consumers who took on mortgages they could not afford and Wall

Street chieftains who loaded up on mortgage-backed securities without regard to the risk,"[1] it was the fiscal policies of the US government that created the conditions for banks and mortgage lenders to behave irresponsibly. What's worse, the government then failed to intervene and make decisions that would have stopped the bleeding.

Let's begin with Bush's political aspirations towards creating an ownership society. In two different 2004 speeches, Bush stated that "we're creating . . . an ownership society in this country, where more Americans than ever will be able to open up their door where they live and say, welcome to my house, welcome to my piece of property."[2] One of the goals behind the ownership society involved enabling working- and middle-class individuals to see themselves as owners of a mortgage, a stock portfolio, a private pension plan, and so on. To create an ownership society, the Bush administration and the Federal Reserve would move to enact fiscal policies that would make it easier for people to become homeowners.

However, this led the government to adopt fiscal policies that would prove disastrous. For example, the Federal Reserve deviated "from the regular way of conducting policy"[3] by creating unusually low interest rates. Over the course of 2001, the Feds lowered interest rates from 6.5% to 1.75%, making it far easier for people to obtain loans.[4] In the summer of 2002, Bush announced his goal of increasing the number of minority homeowners in the US to 5.5 million by 2010 through the of use subsidies, tax credits, and a commitment of $440 billion from GSEs, the Federal National Mortgage Association (FNMA or "Fannie Mae") and the Federal Home Loan Mortgage Corporation (FHLMC, or "Freddie Mac"). The names Fannie Mae and Freddie Mac probably sound familiar; we'll get back to them later.

In the meantime, the Bush administration continued to reform the home-buying process by creating the American Dream Downpayment Initiative (ADDI), which came under the supervision of the US Department of Housing and Development.[5] On top of unusually low interest rates, ADDI further encouraged banks to loosen their loan standards by providing low-income families with down payment assistance of up to

$10,000, while lowering closing costs by nearly $700 per loan.[6] The combined lowering of interest rates, which eventually dropped to 1%, and Bush's commitment to the ownership society led to a boom in new home construction and the purchase of existing homes. Bush's policy seemed to have worked: by 2004, the US Census Bureau found that a record-high 69.2% Americans could be classified as homeowners.[7]

Although noble sounding, the idea that every American has the right to an affordable home turned out to be a nightmare in practice. Home ownership was part of Bush's re-election platform, an attempt to sell his version of the American dream in the hope of political dividends. It had already worked wonders for former British prime minister Margaret Thatcher in the 1980s. By offering "strong incentives to [low-income] residents to buy their council estate flats at reduced rates,"[8] Thatcher transformed a swath of traditionally left-leaning voters into Tory supporters nearly overnight. It's not hard to see why Bush relied on a similar policy: US Republicans have always had difficulty winning the low-income/minority vote, so why not drum up support by offering them affordable housing, even if they couldn't really afford it?

But the government took a big gamble when it allowed Fannie Mae and Freddie Mac to ensure mortgage loans for people who couldn't get them privately. By guaranteeing their loan transactions, the government enabled Fannie Mae and Freddie Mac to operate as private companies but under the protective arm of the government should anyone default on a loan. Fannie Mae and Freddie Mac have also donated hundreds of millions of dollars to politicians in Washington. With so much money on the table, politicians felt an obligation to their "donors" and become susceptible to political manipulation, often sacrificing the needs of the people for the sake of donor support.

Usually, the private sector would never finance such mortgages because the risk of default would be too high. Sound financial transactions depend on an understanding of the risks involved. Without this understanding, anything goes, both for the GSEs, who no longer chanced a loss for risky loans, as well as for unstable homebuyers who had nothing to lose when a down payment wasn't required. Ratings agencies also sweetened the pot by giving mortgage-backed bonds AAA ratings. House prices kept rising since homebuyers, seduced by low-interest loans, were willing to take on massive amounts of debt. With the US government guaranteeing loans, almost anyone could be approved for a mortgage. And so when house costs rose, homeowners took out home equity loans to fund consumption. Household debt quickly got out of hand, with homeowners borrowing and spending far beyond their means. Individual household debt swelled to 134% of disposable income in 2008. In the six-year period between 2001 and 2007, US mortgage debt nearly doubled, with the amount of debt per household rising 63%.[9] All of this happening, mind you, in a job economy in which wages were essentially frozen.

This led to a very fragile situation: more borrowing, more spending, more debt, but literally no income to pay any of it back. Easy access to credit and a rising housing market further encouraged homebuyers to acquire "adjustable interest-rate" subprime mortgages. Adjustable-rate mortgages allowed borrowers to take out loans with below-market interest rates for a certain period of time, after which the interest would readjust to the market rate. But when interest rates returned to normal levels in 2006, the upward trend of the housing market was brought to a screeching halt. Homeowners saw their equity disappearing before their eyes. Those with low incomes found that they could not afford to make their mortgage payments as interest rates rose. As prices started to fall, mortgage-backed securities became increasingly worthless. Ratings agencies removed the high ratings they had granted, and investors who had been lured in by high ratings saw that they didn't actually know what they had invested in.

In my previous book, I suggested that banks needed to be more selective when considering candidates for loans. When criteria are too lenient, people suffer needlessly. We now know that many people did suffer. It turns out that allowing low-income families to purchase homes at "bubble-inflated prices" ultimately "saddle[d] hundreds of thousands of poor families with an unmanageable debt burden."[10] Millions of people suddenly found that their homes were worth less than their mortgages, so they couldn't afford to leave and, with rising interest rates, many couldn't afford to stay. Foreclosures were rampant and neighborhoods full of abandoned homes brought down property values for those still able to maintain their houses.

After the Party, The Crash

The US housing bubble has raised some hard questions, not the least of which is whether everyone should be able to become a homeowner. Because of decades of government policies, many North Americans view home ownership as a right rather than a privilege. Home ownership in Canada recently reached 70%. Yet 30% of Canadian households do not pay income taxes because their earnings are below the low-income threshold. And even though the bulk of those who earn more own a home, that doesn't mean all homeowners are living within their means. Too many of us want a certain lifestyle even if we can't afford it. Young people fresh out of university strive to attain the luxuries their parents enjoyed at the peak of their careers. Rather than living cheaply, paying off debt, and building savings, these young adults plunge into home ownership as soon as a bank will approve a mortgage. But because they may not have learned the habits of saving or considered costs beyond the mortgage payment, they leave themselves vulnerable. Youth is a time of great change and opportunity, and owning a home can hold a person back if he or she is tied to one city and can't take advantage of job offers elsewhere. Of course, the culprit isn't just the impetuousness of youth. People of all ages buy more expensive homes than they can afford and end up with massive debt (or worse) as a result.

In the US, authorities finally seem to be recognizing that the ideal of home ownership should be taken off its pedestal. In March 2011, US Treasury Secretary Timothy Geithner stated that the government should, "at a deliberate pace," pull back from supporting the housing market. In prepared remarks for the Senate Committee on Banking, Housing and Urban Affairs, Geithner asserted that the housing policies of the past decades should be reversed, stating, "our goal is not for every American to become a homeowner." His comments came in reaction to taxpayers bearing the burden for losses in the housing market that had been supported by GSEs like Fannie Mae and Freddie Mac. "Taxpayers," Geithner remarked, were left holding the bag "for much of the risk incurred by a poorly supervised housing finance market."[11]

It's not that Bush didn't try to put the brakes on unsound lending practices, but when he pushed to enact tougher regulations on Fannie Mae and Freddie Mac, Congress blocked him. Along with Bush's top economic officials, blinkered Democrats such as Barney Frank, who infamously announced that the GSEs were not in any financial difficulty, tried to score political points by refusing to acknowledge the instability created by the housing boom and the widespread use of subprime mortgages. Hence, in the wake of other highly publicized government endeavors, such as the "war on terror," the government continued to turn a blind eye to the predatory lending practices that their own policies had facilitated. According to Bush Treasury Secretary John W. Snow, the "administration took a lot of pride that homeownership had reached historic highs. But what we forgot in the process was that it has to be done in the context of people being able to afford their house. We now realize there was a high cost." Likewise, as Bush's chief economic adviser Lawrence B. Lindsay remarks, "there was little impetus to raise alarms about the proliferation of easy credit that was helping Mr. Bush meet housing goals. 'No one wanted to stop that bubble. . . . It would have conflicted with the president's own policies'."[12]

The following years were, and still are, years of anxiety. Early in the financial crisis Fannie Mae and Freddie Mac were taken over by the government. Finally, in October of 2011, steps were taken to relieve some of the burden on troubled homeowners. Fannie Mae and Freddie Mac issued new rules[13] that would allow millions of borrowers who made their payments on time to refinance their high-rate mortgages into lower rate loans. Under this plan, borrowers with loans backed by Fannie Mae or Freddie Mac who owed more on their mortgages than their homes' current value, or who had only a small amount of home equity, would be able to refinance if they had not missed a payment in the previous six months and hadn't had more than one late payment in the preceding year. Although this means the government will collect less interest and see less money returned to it, it's better than the alternative since defaults and foreclosures, which bring down property values for everyone, ultimately end up costing more than refinanced loans. Even so, these new rules are not a magic solution. Only a small percentage of those struggling with their mortgages will qualify for the refinancing plan. The Obama administration's Home Affordable Modification Program (HARP), which began in 2009, was designed to help lower interest rates; but only thirty-thousand homes were refinanced under HARP in its first two years.

Further action, such as reducing the principal balance on loans that have gone under their book value, or the net value of their assets, because of late or uncertain payments, is still needed. But banks are unwilling to accept such losses. Since 2010, the US government has offered private mortgage companies incentives encouraging them to offer principal reduction for troubled borrowers. In January 2012, the Obama administration stated that it would sharply increase the amount of those incentives, partly in an effort to induce the participation of Fannie Mae and Freddie Mac. In July 2012, however, the independent federal agency that administers Fannie Mae and Freddie Mac said that it would not let the mortgage finance companies offer debt forgiveness to homeowners. As a result, too many people have had to learn the hard way that home ownership doesn't guarantee the security and stability promised in the American dream.

The Hangover Felt Around the World

It's tempting to think of the US housing crisis as a domestic issue. Unfortunately, we've learned that the US was not the only country to suffer when the housing bubble finally burst; rather, the housing crisis sent shockwaves throughout the global economy. In the following chapter, I will discuss the effects of globalization in more detail. At this point, it suffices to say that in today's economy, it is more and more common for banks to use savings from foreign sources to provide loans to both households and businesses. And as Henry C. K. Liu points out, an estimated 50% of the money financing the housing bubble via "'securitized' mortgaged debt" was "owned by foreign investors."[14] During the housing boom, foreign banks and investors poured significant capital into US real estate hoping to make big profits from the rising mortgage market. As Federal Reserve Chairman Ben Bernanke points out, "the net inflow of foreign saving to the United States, which was about 1 to $1/_2$ percent of our national output in 1995, reached about 6 percent of national output in 2006, an amount equal to about $825 billion in today's dollars."[15] This massive influx of foreign capital provided the economic means for the Feds to lower interest rates, and the banks and investment firms the freedom to aggressively compete for borrowers by providing cheap credit to both households and businesses. Moreover, the large amount of foreign savings flowing into the US had the effect of lowering returns on long-term investments, such as Treasury Bonds, which led investors to demand investments that promised higher returns but were still considered safe. This provided the impetus for large investment firms to create complex mortgage securities that would fulfill this demand; however, as we have seen, these securities involved significant risks that neither the banks that created them nor the investors that demanded them fully understood.

When US housing prices began to plummet, shocked foreign investors began to pull their capital from the credit markets en masse. With mortgage defaults and delinquencies on the rise and the losses piling up, foreign investment banks, many of which had themselves borrowed millions to jump into the rising US credit and housing markets, reported major losses. In 2008, the International Monetary Fund (IMF) projected that global financial institutions would eventually have to write off $1 trillion of their mortgage-backed securities holdings, with European banks alone suffering roughly $1.6 trillion in losses.[16] Not only did these losses virtually wipe out most of the capital in the world banking system, the banks that survived also stopped lending out of fear of losing even more.[17] As a result, the credit market came to a near standstill. This in turn caused sharp decline in stock prices as investor confidence dropped right along with the housing prices.

In short, the US housing crisis was far from a domestic problem. Given the nature of international finance today, as well as the leading role that the US plays in global economics, the housing crash injected a poison in the veins of the economy, and it was only a matter of time before the rest of the world felt the effects. Since governments, financial institutions, and individuals refused to take the necessary precautions, one country's mistakes became the catalyst for what eventually blossomed into a worldwide recession.

The principal causes that led to the housing crisis in the US—poor government policy, decisions motivated by political calculations rather than sound economic reasoning—render *all* democratic countries vulnerable to similar kinds of crises. Such crises don't happen in a vacuum; ultimately, global economic problems come back to the decisions made by governments and individuals. Confusingly, even after the disaster of the US government-run GSEs, the Conservative government in Canada has recently followed in the footsteps of its southern neighbors by funneling over $600 million of public money into subsidies for the automotive sector and the venture capital business. These sectors have become, for all intents and purposes, "wards of the state." And although the Canadian government has persuaded themselves "that this did not involve the government in 'picking winners'," the fact of the matter is that companies incapable of keeping their own financial houses in order shouldn't be propped up by government money.[18] This creates a corporate welfare system that victimizes both taxpayers and legitimate businesspeople willing to risk their own capital to stimulate economic growth.

Moreover, the decision to subsidize some sectors of the economy rather than others is favoritism at best, cronyism at worst. This kind of economic policy inevitably begs the question of where the money for these subsidies is coming from: businesspeople somewhere else are losing, through no fault of their own, so that proven losers somewhere else can win with government help. As US corporate welfare expert

Terry Buss points out, the money always comes from "'other cities and states'";[19] any corporate welfare scheme inevitably causes governments to place the needs of a select few above national interests. The financial success of any nation hinges on government's capacity to avoiding using political leverage as an excuse to try to control the market. As the example of the US housing bubble shows, the more the government tries to pick economic winners and losers, the more likely they are to make the problem worse, rather than better.

Key Takeaways

- The US housing bubble was the "trigger" to the broader international economic crisis.

- The bubble was caused in part by certain government policies, such as the ownership society. The ownership society refers to the notion that everyone in America, regardless of income, should be able to own their own home.

- The ownership society led the US government to adopt economic policies that opened the door for unusually low-interest rates and banks to relax lending standards, which allowed high-risk borrowers to obtain cheap mortgages backed by GSEs. This produced a temporary boom in the housing market.

- Both investors and the Federal Reserve were far too confident that the housing market was going to continue to rise. The market crashed when high-risk borrowers began to default on their mortgages.

- In recent years, US government authorities have created policies to help mitigate the housing crisis, though recovery has been slow.

- The housing crisis was not only a US problem: because a large part of the housing boom was financed by foreign capital, the crash had negative effects on the global economy as whole.

ENDNOTES

[1] Jo Becker, Sheryl Gay Stolberg, and Stephen Labaton, "White House Philosophy Stoked Mortgage Bonfire," *New York Times*, 20 December 2008. <http://www.nytimes.com/2008/12/21/business/21admin.html?em=&adxnnl=1&adxnnlx=1229887026-rSiHlh3VUrAQb5LnNToHHA&_r=0>

[2] Bush qtd. in "Disowned by the Ownership Society," by Naomi Klein, *The Nation*, 18 February 2008. <http://www.thenation.com/article/disowned-ownership-society>

[3] John B. Taylor, *Getting Off Track: How Government Actions and Interventions Caused, Prolonged, and Worsened the Financial Crisis* (Hoover Institution Press, 2009).

[4] Board of Governors of the Federal Reserve System, "Intended Federal Funds Rate, Change and Level, 1990 to the Present," 26 January 2010. <http://www.federalreserve.gov/monetarypolicy/openmarket.htm>

[5] US Department of Housing and Urban Development, "American Dream Downpayment Initiative," 16 December 2003. <http://www.hud.gov/offices/cpd/affordablehousing/programs/home/addi/>

[6] The White House, President George W. Bush, "President Calls for Expanding Opportunities to Home Ownership," 17 June 2000. <http://georgewbush-whitehouse.archives.gov/news/releases/2002/06/20020617-2.html>

[7] US Census Bureau, "Census Bureau Reports on Residential Vacancies and Homeownership," 26 October 2007. <http://www.census.gov/hhes/www/housing/hvs/qtr307/q307press.pdf>

[8] Ibid.

[9] US Federal Reserve, "Flow of Funds Accounts in the United States," 7 June 2012. <http://www.federalreserve.gov/releases/z1/Current/annuals/a2005-2011.pdf>

[10] Dean Baker, "Bush's House of Cards," *The Nation*, 4 August 2004. <http://www.thenation.com/article/bushs-house-cards>

[11] US Department of the Treasury, "Written Testimony by Secretary Timothy F. Geithner before the House Committee on Financial Services," 1 March 2011. <http://www.treasury.gov/press-center/press-releases/Pages/tg1082.aspx>

[12] Snow and Lindsay qtd. in Becker, Stolberg, Labaton, 2008.

[13] Federal Housing Finance Agency, "FHFA, Fannie Mae and Freddie Mac Announce HARP Changes to Reach More Borrowers," 24 October 2011. <http://www.fhfa.gov/webfiles/22721/HARP_release_102411_Final.pdf>

[14] Liu qtd. in "The Housing Bubble's Impact on the Economy," eFinanceDirectory.com, 26 April 2009. <http://efinancedirectory.com/articles/The_Housing_Bubble's_Impact_on_the_Economy.html>

[15] Ben Bernanke, "Four Questions about the Financial Crisis," Board of Governors of the Federal Reserve System, 14 April 2009. <http://www.federalreserve.gov/newsevents/speech/bernanke20090414a.htm>

[16] Reuters, "US, European Banks Writedowns, Credit Losses [Factbox]," 5 November 2009. <http://www.reuters.com/article/2009/11/05/banks-writedowns-losses-idCNL554155620091105?rpc=44>

[17] *Wikipedia*, "Subprime Mortgage Crisis," N.d. <http://en.wikipedia.org/wiki/Subprime_mortgage_crisis#Financial_market_impacts.2C_2007>

[18] Andrew Coyne, "There Are No Good Reasons for Government Handouts to Corporations," *National Post*, 16 January 2013. <http://fullcomment.nationalpost.com/2013/01/16/andrew-coyne-there-are-no-good-reasons-for-government-handouts-to-manufacturing-sector/>

[19] Buss qtd. in "The Harper Government's Crony Capitalism," by Mark Milke, *Times Colonist*, 25 January 2013. <http://www.timescolonist.com/opinion/columnists/mark-milke-the-harper-government-s-crony-capitalism-1.55969>

Chapter Two

UNDERSTANDING GLOBALIZATION

"Globalization is not something we can hold off or turn off . It is the economic equivalent of a force of nature—like wind or water." – Bill Clinton

AS THE US housing crisis demonstrates, every major financial decision happening today takes place in the context of globalization—the process whereby the world's markets and businesses become increasingly interdependent. As international trade has expanded, and multinational companies have grown larger and more powerful, globalization has come in for its share of criticism. A World Economic Forum survey of twenty-five thousand citizens across twenty-five countries found that, while the majority of survey respondents see globalization as beneficial, they are also concerned that it will have a detrimental impact on the environment, the number and quality of jobs available in their country, the gap between rich and poor, world peace and stability, and workers' rights.[1] To help you understand globalization and its effect on North American citizens, I clarify the pertinent debates and issues surrounding globalization, its benefits and drawbacks, how it affects the labor force in developed countries, and its role in the European debt crisis. Understanding globalization will help you recognize the challenges facing your investment portfolio in an increasingly global marketplace.

What Is Globalization?

We've all heard the term globalization, but what does it mean? The fact is there is no one single agreed-upon definition. Broadly speaking, we can say that globalization describes the set of processes that have increased the connectivity, integration, and communication of trade, investment, peoples, and knowledge across national, political, and cultural boundaries. As David Held and Anthony McGrew put it, globalization is essentially "a widening, deepening and speeding up of worldwide interconnectedness in all aspects of contemporary social life, from the cultural to the criminal, the financial to the spiritual."[2] In essence, however, globalization is the process of deepening international economic integration.

According to a definition established in 2000 by the International Monetary Fund (IMF), globalization has

- increased world trade and transactions;
- increased movements in capital and investment;
- increased migration and movement of people; and
- increased dissemination of knowledge.

All of these aspects of globalization have been assisted by advancements in technology, which have made communication and transportation cheaper and easier, thereby shrinking the cost of international trade and investment.

In economic terms, globalization has led to a deregulation of labor, commodity, and capital markets for the sake of increasing multinational trade, investment, and ownership of assets. The endgame is to provide companies with a competitive advantage by lowering their production costs and allowing them to create or discover investment opportunities through new markets being opened up abroad. But rapid transnational movements of capital, commodities, technology, and labor means that markets have become increasingly interdependent. According to British sociologist Anthony Giddens, a consequence of this increasing interdependence is "that local happenings are shaped by events occurring many miles away and vice versa."[3] Globalization creates a kind of ripple or domino effect. The actions or inactions of one country's government, through the exercise of its legal, economic, political, or military power, can have serious repercussions in communities, nations, and households on an entirely different continent.

The Debt Crisis in Europe

A perfect example of how local events can ripple around the world because of globalization is the European debt crisis, which the head of the Bank of England Sir Mervyn King calls "the most serious financial crisis at least since the 1930s, if not ever."[4]

The European debt crisis basically describes the inability of certain countries—Portugal, Ireland, Italy, Greece, and Spain (sometimes unflatteringly referred to as "PIIGS")—to pay their debts. As a result, these countries are in danger of defaulting on various loans from European banks, which will cause their bonds to plunge in value. If a country defaults on its loan, the ensuing drop in value of its bonds might radically unbalance the debt-to-assets ratio in European banks—that is to say, most of the assets held by European banks would be financed by debt, which would place them in immediate danger should creditors begin demanding repayment. The banks could become insolvent. Because of the global market system, if one European bank goes down others will likely follow, causing a catastrophic chain-reaction for a world banking system already reeling from the 2008 financial crisis.

The European debt crisis began in the wake of the economic recession in the US. Along with external global factors, the PIIGS nations were further destabilized by internal factors, such as uncontrolled government spending and lifetime entitlements for public-sector workers. The situation is particularly dire in Greece. In the years immediately after switching to the Euro, Greece experienced increased gross domestic product (GDP), with the economy growing by 4% a year until 2008. But increased growth masked deeper problems, such as unsustainable budget deficits and increased reliance on foreign borrowing. The Greek government deliberately misreported their actual deficit numbers in order to stay within the European Union's (EU) monetary guidelines. The situation got so bad that the Greek government was forced to reveal the truth, revising their deficit predictions from 3.7% of GDP in early 2009 to 12.7% by the end of that year, and ballooning to 13.6% in 2010.[5] At 13.6% of GDP, Greece's debts exceeded their entire national economy.

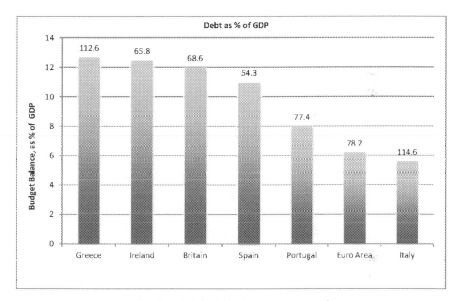

Figure 2–1: Budget balance, as % of GDP
(2009 estimate) + debt as % of GDP

To make matters worse, international investors reacted by pushing for higher returns to compensate for the increased risk of dealing in Greece's bonds. Loss of investor confidence triggered a vicious cycle in which the demand for higher yields raised Greece's borrowing costs, which in turn caused investors to demand even higher yields, and so on. Moreover, because of globalization, loss of investor confidence in one country often contaminates other countries in similar situations, leading investors to pull out of risky situations and reinvest in the most financially stable EU member states.

The result was a US $1 trillion emergency bailout package put together by the IMF. The flow of bailout capital was, however, contingent on PIIGS' commitment to dramatically slash spending through harsh austerity measures and by attempting to increase exports. While austerity seems to make sense in the abstract, increased taxation and decreased spending has resulted in less demand, less growth, and more unemployment. In Greece, the jobless rate has climbed to an eye-popping 23%, with close to 55% of the fifteen-to-twenty-four age demographic out of work, while in Spain the unemployment rate is even higher, registering at 24.6%.[6] At the same time, higher taxes mean that governments in more fiscally responsible EU nations are facing increased anger from their own citizens. In a global economic system, Greece's profligate spending means higher taxes for German and French citizens.

To use a more personal analogy: imagine that you've been financially responsible. You've put money away, you've stayed within your financial means, and you've taken steps to secure your future. Your brother, however, is a spendthrift: when times are good he blows his money on things he can't afford, and he pays for everything with credit cards without caring about interest rates. If your family follows the EU's economic model, you're on the hook for your brother's bad spending habits. But in lending your brother money, you put yourself at risk: despite all the precautions you've taken, the extra burden means that pretty soon you're going to be in debt. And if your brother doesn't change his ways, things might get even worse for both of you. Is this situation fair? No. But if that's the reality, you've got to find some way to deal with it.

But what does this crisis mean for us here in North America? The European crisis is not a problem confined to that continent "over there": a global financial marketplace means that we inevitably feel the tremors from other markets, even ones as far away as Europe. As Canadian finance minister Jim Flaherty points out, although Canadian financial institutions "have a limited exposure to the Greek banking system, . . . global banking is interrelated and shocks in the European banking system can have negative effects" on both Canadian and American banking systems. In January 2012, the Bank of Canada estimated that European debt concerns would cost Canada 0.6% (about $10 billion) in economic output, while the US would lose roughly 0.8% of GDP.[7] What's more, both the US Federal Reserve and the Bank of Canada have been pumping money into the IMF to keep the global financial system functioning. This means that Canadian and American taxpayers *are also on the hook for European debt.* And because the Federal Reserve can make decisions without going through the checks and balances that regulate the branches of the US government, they can simply decide to spend as much tax money as they find necessary, without intervention from the government, without debate, and without voting.

So the Euro family with the free-spending brother is actually a global family. And because of globalization, the contagion of fear that spread across Europe is quite capable of reaching our own shores. We forget this one essential lesson at our own peril: no one is immune.

Globalization: A Force for Good or Evil?

The European debt crisis raises serious questions about the nature of globalization, and whether the deregulation of markets has been a force for good or evil. Here, my focus is primarily on the positive and negative effects of economic globalization: governmental, geographical, and cultural factors affecting your wealth are addressed in other parts of this book. Learning how to assess and evaluate the effects of globalization will enable you to grasp how your money can work smarter within the current global-economic climate.

A Force for Good?

Despite the criticisms against globalization, economists point to a number of benefits stemming from the worldwide interdependence globalization brings. In a paper for the IMF, David Dollar and Aart Kraay[8] identify at least three positive economic effects of globalization.

1. **Accelerated GDP Growth:** Countries that take a globalized approach to business have experienced an accelerated growth rate of per capita GDP. As the following chart demonstrates, developing and non-globalized countries fared much worse over the same period of time. Cross-border capital now accounts for almost 15% of global GDP, up from 3% at the turn of the nineteenth century.

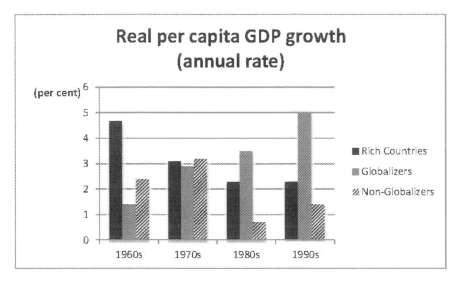

Figure 2–2: Real per capita GDP growth (annual rate)

2. **Shared Growth Benefits:** At least in theory, globalization is a two-way street. Everyone benefits when countries specialize in exporting the products that they are most efficient at creating. If Germans make the best car transmissions in the most cost-efficient way, the Swiss make the best tires, the US manufactures the most cost-efficient steel, and South Africa the most cost-efficient assembly lines, the consumer gets the best car for the cheapest price. What's more, the parts contributed by each country for the vehicle increase in trade value. The rapid increase of manufacturing in markets abroad also generates a high demand for certain kinds of commodities in different markets around the world, while the combination of lower prices for imports and higher prices for exports can boost

the disposable income per capita in both developing and developed countries. In Canada, for instance, the combination of low-import and high-export costs has increased real disposable income per capita 8.5% over the last five years. This low-import/high-export dynamic of global trade helps create "healthier corporate balance sheets and continued improvement in government fiscal positions."[9]

3. **Narrows the Gap Between Rich and Poor:** Evidence suggests that globalization plays an important role in narrowing the gap between developed and developing nations. Only twenty years ago, countries such as China, Bangladesh, and India were among the poorest nations in the world. After taking steps towards greater participation in the global economy, these countries now boast a significant increase in per capita income. Further integration of poorer countries into the world economy provides opportunities for these countries not only to catch up to richer nations, but also for the richer nations themselves to increase trade opportunities and strengthen market competition

A Force for Evil?

While globalization has had positive effects in those countries willing to seize the opportunities available in an expanding marketplace, it has also had its fair share of drawbacks.

- **Widening Disparity:** Despite accelerated GDP and income growth, the gap between the richest and poorest countries actually seems to be growing. Rich countries are trading almost exclusively with other rich countries: over 80% of international finance capital flows between US, Western European, and East Asian countries—not between rich countries and lesser developed nations. Even more troubling is the widening disparity between rich and poor within developed countries. The Organization for Economic Development and Co-operation's 2007 Employment Outlook points out that, in Canada, the share of labor income relative to GDP has dropped over the last twenty years.[10] The North American middle class is fast disappearing. Jobs that once provided the financial means for working-class aspirations—home, retirement, college funds for the kids—have been replaced by lower paying work. In order to fulfill these aspirations with reduced pay, families are going into increased credit debt, and banks are loaning money to those who can't afford to pay it back. A survey conducted by the US Census Bureau shows that one in six Americans now live in poverty, while the richest 20% of the US population controls 84% of the wealth.[11]

Statistics such as these have led to social unrest, which has manifested on both the left and the right sides of the political spectrum. In September 2011, the Occupy Wall Street protest called attention to the radical disparity between the wealthiest 1% and the other 99%; on the conservative end, the Tea Party movement advocates protectionist, pro-domestic employment strategies that cut down on the increased migration of people. Despite their ideological differences, both the Occupy Wall Street and Tea Party movements are populist responses to the growing wealth disparity that has emerged in an era of increasing globalization.

- **Increased Market Volatility:** In theory, the opening up of markets allows for increased productivity and the reallocation of capital from less productive businesses to more productive ones. But as markets become more and more interdependent, they also become more and more fragile, susceptible to sudden collapses that can have widespread effects. If a collapse in one segment of the market occurs, it can become contagious, infecting other segments of the market in a chain-effect that threatens even the most successful businesses. We have already seen an example of increased market volatility in the effects of the European debt crisis.

- **Rising Unemployment:** While the increased presence of multinational corporations can lead to the long-term improvement of education, living conditions, and financial health of many countries, they can also bring short-term spikes in unemployment. Two major factors have led to rising unemployment in a globalized economy:

- *Outsourcing:* Corporations often try to cut costs by outsourcing jobs, contracting goods and services from less developed countries at a lower cost.
- *Automation:* The appearance of multinationals hastens the shift from manual labor power to automation. Though businesses become more technologically advanced and efficient, automation also reduces the need for unskilled or undereducated workers, thus raising unemployment levels.

Like many aspects of globalization, outsourcing and automation look different depending on your point of view. Although they have generated troubling consequences for the job market in developed countries, both outsourcing and automation have benefitted consumers, working in tandem to exploit our desires for lower prices and cheaper products.

Globalization's Collateral Damage

In North America, the working- and middle-class have become used to a certain standard of living. But in today's society, the modest middle-class goals of having a good job, a decent home, an education, and a bit of extra money set aside for the twilight years are often twisted in advertising and the media, which instead offer golden visions of luxury and plentitude that, frankly, most couldn't possibly afford. Knowing that we're fortunate enough to live in relatively wealthy societies, advertisers repeatedly tell the middle-class that they should expect to have it all.

But this expectation can go two ways. First, many people might believe that they deserve luxury goods and become willing to fund their desires with borrowed money, an attitude that creditors are more than willing to encourage. And, second, people might expect to get the things they want for bargain-basement prices. We're all happy to get a bargain; consumers are demanding lower prices more regularly as we collectively recognize that we live in tough economic times. But to buy the things that we desire at the prices we want, we need them made cheaply. The cost of labor must be much lower than what the law allows in wealthier countries such as ours. So we outsource labor to countries where people will work for a lot less. We rely on cheap labor to satisfy our demand for cheap products.

Look at the relationship between the US and China, for example. China's entrance into the World Trade Organization in 2001 has increased trade between the two countries, with a huge, even disastrous, impact on workers in the US and the country's domestic economy. Between 2001 and 2007, estimates put the number of jobs lost or displaced in the US at 2.3 million, and those losses have not been recouped. Even though workers who could have worked in manufacturing or trade industries might have found work elsewhere, they won't earn as much as before. The lost jobs are the ones that made it possible for people in past generations to live a comfortable working- or middle-class lifestyle without anything more than a high school education. Without these jobs, people resort to lower paying work, such as retail.

The low cost of labor in less developed countries has also made it more difficult for workers to demand higher wages. The consequences extend beyond manufacturing and trade-related jobs. Again, the people hit hardest are those lacking higher education or other credentials. Globalization and advances in technology have made it possible to replace workers with machines or cheaper labor overseas, so today a person really cannot find a good job without higher education. By importing goods, we have displaced goods that would have been made in (and provided jobs in) the US. Outsourcing also encourages multinational corporations to avoid taxation or wait until a generous tax holiday makes it more attractive to bring their money back to North America. Currently, the corporate tax code in the US taxes foreign profits only on money returned to America, at which point the corporations receive a credit for foreign taxes paid on their profits. Yet this still isn't enough; large corporations have been advocating for a territorial tax system, claiming it would help keep them remain competitive. But such a system would eliminate federal taxes on foreign profits so companies would have even more to gain by moving jobs and investments overseas.

One of the byproducts of increased outsourcing has been nothing less than the disappearance of the North American middle-class. Typically, the presence of a stable middle-class means a healthy economy: the middle-class provides a stable consumer base that allows business owners to make investments and create jobs. In North America, the promotion of the middle-class values of hard work, desire for self-improvement, and entrepreneurial spirit have historically helped drive economic productivity. Where the lower-classes are preoccupied with day-to-day survival, the middle-class have both the time and inclination to come up with innovative ideas and start businesses. Yet, job loss or scarcity due to increased outsourcing has eroded the monetary and social rewards that such values used to provide. Both the number and the quality of jobs available to the middle-class have steadily eroded. As a result, many middle-class families have financially "leveraged" themselves, racking up mortgages and massive credit card debts that, as State University of New York finance professor William Raynor surmises, brings them "within a whisker of being pushed off a financial cliff. The continuation of outsourcing jobs overseas may be the final gust of wind that does it for many of them."[12]

The problem is not limited to the middle-class itself; if the middle-class forms the basis for economic health, a disappearing middle class also means the disappearance of a healthy economy. And because of the global reach of today's markets, if the North American middle-class fares badly, it will have negative effects throughout the entire global economy.

The fact is we now live in a global village. Governments and businesses must promote policies that discourage multinational corporations from moving their wealth and jobs overseas. They must put their efforts into education to make North America more competitive and innovative. Still, we cannot simply rely on governments and companies to do all the work for us: jobs for unskilled workers won't magically reappear with better policy decisions. Lower cost labor can be readily found in developing countries, and multinationals will always take advantage of this fact. But a proportionate increase in demand for higher skilled labor in developed countries provides an opportunity for workers willing to take the initiative to upgrade their skills and avoid becoming a casualty of outsourcing and automation. Canada, for example, is now experiencing a shortage of skilled workers both in the trades and in professional areas such as computer science and engineering. In a speech to a Canada–US business group in November 2012, Prime Minister Stephen Harper noted that "'for whatever reason we know that peoples' choices, in terms of the education system, tend to lead us to what appears to be a chronic shortage of certain skills'."[13] By actively promoting the trades or making more apprenticeships available, the government could alleviate this chronic shortage of skilled workers by providing incentives to stay in Canada.

In the absence of such reforms, some have suggested that granting labor unions, traditionally staunch defenders of working-class rights, an expanded role might help protect jobs at home and curb the negative effects of globalization. However, unions may be doing more harm than good.

Globalization and Labor Unions

With rising unemployment and wealth disparity, the role of labor unions might seem more important than ever. After all, if jobs are being lost to low-wage workers elsewhere, shouldn't unions in richer nations do even more to protect the rights of workers within their own country? And doesn't the rise in unemployment mean that the deregulation of trade and labor markets isn't working?

The answer to these questions is a qualified yes and an emphatic NO. Although labor unions tend to support the anti-globalization movement, any attempt to block the effects of globalization risks being marginalized as a nuisance or irrelevant. Instead of resisting globalization, the key is to evolve and adapt with it. Further on, I discuss one such evolution in the collective bargaining strategy adopted by Canadian auto-parts billionaire Frank Stronach. For the present moment, however, the important point is that Stronach ultimately convinced the union at his Magna International auto-parts manufacturing plants to eschew an adversarial approach to collective bargaining. Instead, to borrow the words of globalization and union researcher Michael Walton, Stronach entered into a cooperative agreement that allowed the workers to participate directly in the global success of the company, thus simultaneously "'increasing productivity gains," while "ensuring fairness and . . . protecting reasonable working conditions'."[14]

Union membership rates are actually down in both the US and Canada. Why? The reasons for declining union membership are undoubtedly complex and varied. Nonetheless, part of the problem has to do with the fact that, in many cases, enforced labor regulations have stifled innovation, and unions have unwittingly become one of the *causes* of jobs shifting to lower cost markets. Let's look at a few recent examples.

- **Caterpillar Inc. vs. Canadian Autoworkers Union:** In 2011, the Canadian Autoworkers Union (CAW) entered into a bitter labor dispute with American heavy-equipment manufacturer Caterpillar Inc. The fight was over proposed changes to the company's existing employment terms at their London, Ontario, locomotive plant. Changes included significant cuts to pay and benefits, with some employees' wages dropping almost 55% from $34 to $16.50 per hour. Union leaders interpreted these proposals as examples of simple corporate greed, citing Caterpillar's $5 billion in profits and the $5 million in tax breaks the company received in the Canadian government's 2008 budget. On the corporate side, Caterpillar spokespersons argued that the "'unsustainable cost structure of the operation'" required that the two sides "'negotiate a new, competitive agreement'" that would bring Canadian wages in line with the average pay at US-based plants.[15]

Negotiations eventually broke down in December 2011 when the CAW rejected Caterpillar's offer, voting to strike if a deal could not be reached by January 1. Instead, Caterpillar elected to lock out the plant's employees. The lockout lasted only a month before the company decided to close the London plant and move its operations to a new factory in Muncie, Indiana. Nearly five-hundred workers lost their jobs because of the plant closure. Though the media construed Caterpillar's actions as heartless and greedy, the union's decision not to take the company's offer and threaten to strike sealed the plant's fate. The union's attempt to play hard ball with a deep-pocketed multinational corporation sporting an aggressive global investment strategy was bound to fail. Rather than protect their workers by encouraging them to make sacrifices while demonstrating to management their understanding of the issues and looking for compromise, the union decided to bet all or nothing. Predictably, they ended up with nothing.

- **Boeing vs. National Labor Relations Board:** Another example of a union's failure to grasp the economic implications of globalization can be found in the 2011 conflict between US-based aircraft manufacturer Boeing and the National Labor Relations Board (NLRB). Acting on a complaint by the Machinists and Aerospace Workers union, the NLRB filed a lawsuit claiming that Boeing had illegally moved production of its new $1-billion 787 passenger jet from unionized factories in Washington state to non-unionized plants in South Carolina. The NLRB's lawyers claimed that Boeing's decision was retaliation against the union for exercising its legal right to strike, whereas Boeing's representatives stated that lower production costs were the main reason behind the move. However, the union convinced the NLRB to drop the lawsuit once Boeing agreed to a contract extension that included higher wages, increased provisions for job security, and expanded jet production using unionized labor in Washington state.[16]

The dropped lawsuit averted financial disaster for Boeing, but the NLRB's actions may have triggered something far worse: the increased outsourcing of jobs overseas. The function of the NLRB is to arbitrate labor disputes fairly, making sure that both sides legally stay "in bounds." But in carrying forward the lawsuit against Boeing, the NLRB tried to score political points by punishing Boeing for moving production to a state where unions don't carry as much influence. Unlike Washington, South Carolina is a right-to-work state, meaning that workers are not obligated to join a union or pay union dues. By moving production to a right-to-work state, Boeing effectively used an outsourcing strategy within American borders. Yet, unlike overseas outsourcing, Boeing's strategy was intended to help create jobs within the US itself. The NLRB's politically motivated lawsuit serves as a warning to other large unionized US companies: invest in right-to-work states, and we'll sue. This attitude actively discourages companies from investing in the domestic economy and creating jobs for fear of union backlash. Moreover, recent studies show that investment in right-to-work states has had a net positive effect on the health of the US economy, as right-to-work states boast reduced unemployment and a lower cost of living than states with a strong union presence.[17] As one editorialist in the *Wall Street Journal* sums it up, "the ability of the 21 right-to-work states . . . to attract businesses from pro-union states will . . . be eroded [by the NLRB's actions]. The AFL-CIO may cheer that message, but in practice the result is likely to be that more companies simply send jobs overseas where there's no NLRB. Congratulations."[18]

- **Wisconsin vs. Collective Bargaining:** In the past, unions played an important role in protecting workers from exploitation by greedy industrialists. Now, powerful unions often protect their members at the cost of exacerbating the current fiscal crisis, strong-arming weak local and state governments to accept high-cost defined-benefit pension plans at the taxpayer's expense. The result? Unions are off-loading a significant financial burden onto taxpayers and inflating already-strained state budgets. According to figures released by the Economic Policy Institute in 2011, the generous benefit and compensation plans granted to union employees in non-right-to-work states result in a higher cost of living in those states. What these figures also show is that *states without right-to-work laws actually have a higher rate of unemployment than right-to-work states.* Strained budgets, deficits, higher cost of living, higher unemployment, and even expanded outsourcing are the true cost of unions in today's global economy.

In February 2011, Republican governor Scott Walker decided to take action against unions who put their own sense of entitlement ahead of the financial well-being of the state. Walker proposed what became known as the "Wisconsin Budget Repair Bill." The Bill's intention was to address a projected $3.6-billion deficit by placing limits on union rights—including collective bargaining, compensation, retirement, health insurance, and sick leave—among public-sector employees. Employees were also to become more fiscally responsible by contributing more of their own salaries to pay for health care and pension benefits. The Bill also gave union employees limited right-to-work options, including allowing members to opt out of paying union fees. After heated public debate, which included mass protests at the State Capitol, an unsuccessful union-led bid to oust Governor Walker by recall, and intimidation tactics that saw unions threatening small businesses with boycotts, the Bill passed into law by the Wisconsin Supreme Court.[19]

The debate surrounding Wisconsin's Budget Repair Bill reveals a clash between the states' need for fiscal restraint and the union's desire to protect entrenched privilege. On the one hand, the Bill seeks to positively counter the effects of the global economic recession by demanding a return to fiscally responsible practices at the state level, practices in which unions must play their part. The unions' refusal to do so, coupled with their thuggish behavior towards members of their own community, suggests that unions in developed countries are far more interested in looking out for their own interests than making a few sacrifices for the financial good of everyone. I believe that the Wisconsin Bill should be an example for national, state, and local governments all over the world. Adopting similar policies will curb union influence and go some way toward unions that no longer abuse their rights and stifle innovation.

There's an old saying that power corrupts. With increased power, unions have also become increasingly corrupted and out of step with global economic reality. For all their talk about solidarity, recent events show that unions act like any other lobby or special-interest group: selfishly, ruthlessly, and with a sense of entitlement blind to interests other than their own. Unions may still have an important role to play in the future, but unless they evolve and adapt to meet the demands of a globalized society, they will only contribute further instability.

Beyond the Union: Frank Stronach and Magna International

Canadian business magnate and auto-parts billionaire Frank Stronach has introduced one of the more successful solutions to many of the problems corroding the union management relationship today. As founder and long-time chairman of Magna International, a major force in global automotive parts manufacturing based in Aurora, Ontario, Stronach has been notoriously resistant to unionizing his workers. Instead, Magna International developed a unique strategy for including workers in a profit-sharing scheme, or "entrepreneurial compensation system," in which the company sets aside 10% of pre-tax profit for their employees. This means that if the company does well, so does its employees.

Still, in 2007, the CAW finally signed an agreement to unionize workers at Magna. Stronach and then-union boss Buzz Hargrove announced a deal that obliged the CAW to change its approach to the collective bargaining process, as well as to the accepted hierarchies of unionized workplaces. For example, the CAW was forced to give up the use of shop stewards, the worker-elected representatives for each department that deal with management on behalf of employees. Instead, the CAW and Stronach agreed to a single employee advocate for the entire plant, thereby minimizing the potential for stewards to set themselves against management. This meant a radical restructuring of the relationship not only between unions and management, but also of employees among themselves.

Stronach prefers an approach in which everyone—employees, management, executives, stakeholders, and so on—is in the same boat together. Creative solutions such as these may lead to far more economically productive worker-management relationships in which employees and management become partners in their own success.

Globalization's Mixed Blessing: Possible Solutions

We can't undo globalization; for better or worse, it's here to stay. To be sure, the news isn't as bad as some, particularly those on the left, make it out to be. If globalization is here to stay, then positive changes can only come from within the pro-business, pro-capitalist mandates that constitute the very foundation of a truly global economy. The ability to change comes down to, on the one hand, taking a good hard look in the global mirror—that is to say, a good look at what policies, behaviors, and beliefs got the PIIGS countries, unions, and workers into trouble in the first place. On the other hand, positive changes also come down to the rational choices individuals, businesses, and governments will have to make to cope with the economic reality of globalization. In its most positive light, globalization emerges from a spirit of cooperation, fairness, inclusion, and a desire for global prosperity. But lack of personal, business, and governmental responsibility has led to a global economy that leads to unsustainable growth. Being a leader in each of these domains means taking an active role in recognizing that increased responsibility is in our own best interests.

The essential question is how better to coordinate global finance and global trade in the twenty-first century. We can take encouragement from the thought that many of the problems of globalization can be solved from within the framework of globalization itself. For Nobel prize-winning economist Joseph Stiglitz, the solution to globalization is more—and better—globalization.[20] The flaw is not globalization itself, but how governments and businesses have implemented it. According to Stiglitz, when cultural and political programs move more in line with the overarching economic demands of globalization, better and fairer financial practices will win the day: freer trade, more transparency in international finance (less corruption), debt forgiveness (creditors must take responsibility for irresponsible lending practices), and more democracy (rule of law, more government transparency). However, even Stiglitz admits that the road won't be an easy one. But since globalization is our reality, we must take the appropriate steps, like upgrading our skills or tempering our consumer demands, to accepting globalization's effects on our financial well-being.

Key Takeaways

- Globalization can be identified by the following four attributes: increased world trade and transactions; increased movements in capital and investment; increased migration and movement of people, and; increased dissemination of knowledge.

- Global interconnectedness creates a ripple or domino effect: the actions of one country's government can have serious repercussions for communities around the world.

- Because of globalization's ripple effect, the European debt crisis can and does affect North American markets, government policies, and even your taxes.

- Two consequences of globalization, outsourcing and automation, have had a profound impact on the North American labor force.

- The traditional strategies employed by labor unions no longer provide an adequate response to the realities of the globalization.

- Magna International's "entrepreneurial compensation system" better reflects the nature of how labor-management relations must evolve to meet the demands of a global marketplace.

- Globalization is not a lost cause: with better government and corporate policies, globalization can lead to better and fairer economic practices that benefit everyone.

ENDNOTES

[1] World Economic Forum, "People Around the World Increasingly Favor Globalization but Worry about Jobs, Poverty and Environment," 1 February 2002. <http://www.globescan.com/news_archives/press_inside.html>

[2] David Held and Anthony McGrew, *Global Transformations: Politics, Economics, and Culture* (Stanford University Press, 1999).

[3] Anthony Giddens, *The Consequences of Modernity* (Stanford University Press, 1990).

[4] Gabriella Griffith, "Mervyn King: 'The World Has Changed'," *London Loves Business*, 7 October 2011. <http://www.londonlovesbusiness.com/business-news/mervyn-king-the-world-has-changed/704.article>

[5] *The Economist*, "A Very European Crisis" (Editorial), 4 February 2010. <http://www.economist.com/node/15452594>

[6] George Georgiopoulis, "Greek Unemployment Rate Soars to New Record, More Pain Ahead," *Financial Post*, 9 August 2009. <http://business.financialpost.com/2012/08/09/greek-unemployment-rate-soars-to-new-record-more-pain-ahead>

[7] Julian Beltrame, "Greece Debt Crisis: Canada May Be Hit with Fallout from Eurozone, Flaherty Says," *Huffington Post*, 16 May 2012. <http://www.huffingtonpost.ca/2012/05/16/greece-debt-crisis-canada-flaherty_n_1522087.html>

[8] David Dollar and Aart Kraay, "Trade, Growth, and Poverty," International Monetary Fund, September 2001. <http://www.imf.org/external/pubs/ft/fandd/2001/09/dollar.htm>

[9] Mark Carney, "The Implications of Globalization for the Economy and Public Policy," Bank of Canada, 18 February 2008. <http://www.bankofcanada.ca/2008/02/speeches/implications-globalization-economy-public-policy/>

[10] Ibid.

[11] Paul Harris, "The Decline and Fall of the Middle Class," *The Guardian*, 13 September 2011. <http://www.guardian.co.uk/commentisfree/cifamerica/2011/sep/13/american-middle-class-poverty>

[12] William Raynor, "Global Outsourcing and the Disappearing Middle Class," *New Work Opinion*, 2003. <http://www.newwork.com/Pages/Opinion/Raynor/Middle%20Class.html>

[13] Harper qtd. in "Lack of Skilled Labour Threatens Canadian Economy, Prime Minister Stephen Harper Says," by Les Whittington, *Toronto Star*, 19 November 2012. <http://www.thestar.com/news/canada/2012/11/19/lack_of_skilled_labour_threatens_canadian_economy_prime_minister_stephen_harper_says.html>

[14] Walton qtd. in "Labor Unions and Globalization," University of Iowa Centre for International Finance and Development, N.d. <http://ebook.law.uiowa.edu/ebook/issues/globalization/reading-table/labor-unions>

[15] Rachel Mendleson, "Electro-Motive Lockout: Caterpillar to Close London Plant, Company Says," *Huffington Post*, 3 February 2012. <http://www.huffingtonpost.ca/2012/02/03/electro-motive-lockout-ca_n_1252510.html>

[16] Steven Greenhouse, "Labor Board Drops Case Against Boeing After Union Reaches Accord," *New York Times*, 9 December 2011. <http://www.nytimes.com/2011/12/10/business/labor-board-drops-case-against-boeing.html>

[17] Robert Barro, "Unions vs. the Right to Work," *Wall Street Journal*, 28 February 2011. <http://online.wsj.com/article/SB10001424052748704150604576166011983939364.html>

[18] *Wall Street Journal*, "The NLRB's Boeing Sham" (Editorial), 12 December 2011. <http://online.wsj.com/article/. doi:SB10001424052970203833104577070572768248242.html>

[19] Ibid., "Wisconsin Unions Get Ugly" (Editorial), 16 April 2011. <http://online.wsj.com/article/SB10001424052748703806304576232780047736062.html>

[20] Joseph Stiglitz, *Making Globalization Work* (W. W. Norton & Co., 2007).

Chapter Three

THE END OF GEOGRAPHY AND THE RISE OF ENVIRONMENTALISM

*"Geography doesn't simply begin and end with maps. . . .
No—geography poses fascinating questions about who we
are and how we got to be that way." – Kenneth C. Burke*

WE CAN'T HELP where we're born; that much is obvious. But does this mean the place in which we're born determines our character and, ultimately, our economic prosperity? Does geography still count in a globally integrated economy, in which capital passes seamlessly through all physical boundaries? And where does the environment figure into all this?

Geographers and economists alike have debated these questions for some time. Such issues are complex, and I certainly don't propose to completely disentangle them here. Regardless of where one stands on these issues, however, it's undeniable that geography plays an important role in shaping the economies of a country or region. For our purposes, geography here refers to a number of interrelated factors that impact a region's economy, such as climate, location, natural resources, as well as the spatial organization of the economic activities within a country, continent, or region. In recent years, an academic sub-discipline has emerged that deals specifically with these kinds of phenomena: economic geography. Economic geography studies where economic activities are located, how they are distributed, and how they are organized in geographic space. This chapter will, among other things, serve as a basic introduction to issues important to economic geographers, including questions about how globalization changes the way economists think about the nature and function of geographical space. The chapter will also look at controversial topics such as the modern environmental movement, the Alberta oil sands, and natural resource-based projects like the Keystone XL pipeline. In an increasingly globalized economy, economic geography provides a valuable tool for broadening our perspective, helping us to understand how closely, and precariously, our economic activities are tied to the places that we live and work.

What Is Economic Geography?

While most of us have heard of a term like globalization, it's less likely that many of us would be familiar with an academic sub-discipline like economic geography. According to Washington University professor Gunter Krumme, economic geography refers "to the way in which individuals and enterprises organize their economic activities in space." Economic geographers thus "study the principles governing the spatial allocation of resources and the resulting consequences." More specifically, economic geography focuses on

- the "location and spatial distribution of economic activities, including questions of 'place,' 'locality,' . . . and land use";
- "exchange, trade, transportation, migration, information and capital flows, [and] communication networks"; and
- "regional growth or decline, technological innovation, . . . regional economic development, etc."[1]

We can already see how economic geography becomes especially important in an increasingly globalized world, which has also dramatically changed our economic, cultural, and political understanding of space and place. Hence, one of the core issues linking globalization with economic geography centers on how we understand the nature of space: has the "frictionless" movement of capital brought about by globalization trumped actual, physical geography? Or does physical geographical space still play a role in determining global economic activity?

Rethinking Geography

For some economic geographers, one of the most prominent features of increased globalization is that it brings about the so-called "death of distance"—that is, in a world in which information technology allows capital to be moved around the world seemingly without constraint, actual physical distance is no longer a hindrance to economic success. In the early 1990s, when globalization was the hot new topic in academic circles, British economist Richard O'Brien famously pronounced that "global financial integration" had effectively brought about the "end of geography"; "geographical location no longer matters in finance or matters much less than hitherto. . . . [M]oney, being fungible, will continue to try to avoid and will largely succeed in escaping the confines of geography."[2] As O'Brien points out, capital is not something material, has very little to do with the paper that a bill is printed on or the metal upon which the queen's likeness happens to be stamped. Rather, capital is "an item of information," and hence, "money is shaped by the development and adoption of information and communication technologies (ICTs)."[3] The future of finance lies, therefore, in developing ICTs that will increasingly manage and regulate information flows. The end of geography thesis was understood to be one of the major triumphs of contemporary capitalism, which would radically decrease the significance of geographical barriers as factors in determining economic success.

Yet, in 2009, O'Brien revisited his earlier views, writing that global capital's tendency to bypass geography had in fact played a crucial role in creating the 2008 financial crisis. O'Brien lists three major links between the end of geography and the ensuing crisis:

- The integration and deregulation of the global marketplace made it much too easy to bundle financial products into complex and obscure packages whose risk, because difficult to assess, resulted in products being mispriced or undervalued. This, in turn, made them easy to sell to investors all over the world, which exacerbated the spread of toxic assets.

- Financial institutions had become over-reliant on what specialists call "wholesale" funding. Traditionally, banks are funded by core-demand deposits made by individual customers and businesses in the institution's geographical locale or demographic market. With the emergence of ICTs and the ability to move money electronically across borders, however, financial institutions have increasingly sought wholesale funding from foreign and brokered deposits, or deposits "received through a broker who takes their wealthy clients' money and finds several different banks in which to deposit it, in order for those clients to receive FDIC [Federal Deposit Insurance Corporation] insurance (and hopefully a more attractive rate)."[4] But when the credit crunch happened and the debt markets shut down due to a lack of investor confidence, the wholesale market dried up, and so did the liquidity of the financial institutions that depended on them.

- The ease and speed of ICT-facilitated global transactions resulted in increasing amounts of financial decisions being made on near blind trust rather than actual knowledge. In turn, when financiers realized the extent to which they were relying on trust rather than a solid understanding of who they were dealing with, a complete collapse in trust followed. As O'Brien puts it, "relationships over a distance in knowledge and culture can be particularly fragile, [and al]though in some respects geography doesn't matter a great deal—a bust bank is a bust bank."[5]

As a result, in recent years economists have begun to reevaluate the importance of physical geography to global finance. As business guru John Kay puts it, the financial crisis showed us that, in many respects, "geography is still important," and that globalization "has not diminished the economic significance of location."[6] With the expansion of markets beyond national borders, those countries or regions that harbor certain geographical advantages, such as an abundance and diversity of natural resources, large and varied territories, and relatively moderate climates, stand to profit through transnational trade by supplying valuable commodities like oil, timber, natural gas, hydroelectric power, precious metals, minerals, and so on. Such advantages typically foster economic growth, although, as I discuss later in this chapter, this isn't always the case in certain parts of the world.

In a perfect world, every corner of the globe would have enough natural resources to sustain itself and would be capable of managing those resources responsibly. Unfortunately, this isn't the case: some regions thrive economically because of geographical advantages, while others struggle. Only a select few regions have been lucky enough, historically and politically, to be situated in places with resources capable of bestowing significant economic benefits. In what follows, I discuss a few examples of the lucky and the not-so-lucky.

The Lucky

- **Canada:** As the world's second largest country, Canada's vast size makes it geographically diverse, with the Appalachian and Rocky mountain ranges and interior plains in the west, the Great Lakes and St. Lawrence lowlands in the east, and the vast rock base of the Canadian shield extending across the northern parts of most provinces. In investment terms, Canada boasts a "diversified portfolio," and as any knowledgeable financial planner will tell you, that's a good thing.

  Economically, Canada greatly benefits from this geographic diversity. The presence of mountains, farmland, freshwater lakes, inland seaways, and large coastal regions has allowed Canada to manufacture and export everything from beef to wheat to oil and hydroelectric power. According to Statistics Canada, natural resources made up nearly 58% of Canada's total exports in 2009.[7]

Due to climate and soil conditions, less than 7% of Canada's total land area is dedicated to farmland; yet agriculture still produces enough grain to meet the nation's food requirements and export surplus to the US.[8] Although much of the country's best farmland for grain and cattle-production is concentrated in the southern part of the prairie provinces (Alberta, Saskatchewan, and Manitoba), the Great Lakes–St. Lawrence river regions of Ontario and Quebec also boast rich and diverse agricultural products that serve large nearby urban centers, including beef cattle, poultry, eggs, grains, and tobacco. On the east coast, the Maritime provinces specialize in a variety of fruit and potato crops, as well as fishing. Large forests on the west coast and across the Canadian Shield have also allowed Canada to become one of the world's leading producers of lumber and timber.[9]

Perhaps the most important natural resources for Canada at the moment are mining and energy products. While agriculture, fishing, and forestry combined make up roughly 2% of Canada's national GDP, mining contributes 4%. Due to the great diversity of materials available—Canada is a top producer of almost sixty different minerals—Canadian mining has become a multi-billion dollar industry.[10] Rising energy demands both at home and abroad, along with rich energy resources, has vaulted Canada to the forefront of crude oil, natural gas, petroleum, hydroelectricity, and uranium production. In 2007, energy products "contributed 5.6% to the GDP and $90 billion in exports."[11] Canada, and not the Middle East, provides the US with the most oil: as of 2010, Canada accounted for roughly 16% of the US's oil imports and 14% of its natural gas.[12] According to the *CIA World Factbook*, Canada now trails only Saudi Arabia and Venezuela in proven oil reserves.[13]

Equally important is the fact that Canada's geographic location renders it almost immune from major natural hazards, such as hurricanes, earthquakes, volcanoes, monsoons, and tsunamis, which afflict other parts of the world. Though inclement weather affects parts of the country from time to time, resource development has been relatively unaffected by poor weather (with the exception of the extreme north). Add the fact that Canada shares the world's largest, unprotected border and trades extensively with the most economically powerful country on the planet, and it's easy to see that Canadians are extremely fortunate to live where they live.

In addition, the diversity and abundance of Canada's natural resources has helped Canadians weather the 2007–2012 series of financial crises. As was to be expected, when the recession hit, commodity prices fell and, in 2008, oil prices dropped from $137 to $35 per barrel between July and December.[14] However, a 2011 report by Natural Resources Canada showed that, while "industrial demand for natural gas plummeted 8.4% in the US," by 2009, "Canadian industrial demand proved to be much more resilient and only fell by 1%."[15] Commodity prices have nearly returned to pre-recession levels, an upward trend that kept the recession short for Canada. And since both energy demands and prices are again on the rise, Canada's oil and gas reserves grant the country unprecedented bargaining power in the global energy trade. Basically, Canada possesses resources that everyone else in the world wants, a nice position to be in both strategically and economically

- **The United States:** Despite the economic problems plaguing the US in recent years, the country still reaps many advantages from a favorable economic geography. Like Canada, one of the most important aspects of US geography is space, which Robert H. Wiebe calls "the most powerful influence in the shaping of American society."[16] The continental US is the fourth largest country in the world, only slightly smaller than Canada, and about half the size of Russia. As a result, the US similarly benefits from a diversity of geographic regions, and thus shares a similar list of natural resources with its northern neighbors, including uranium, gold, iron, nickel, natural gas, and timber. The US also holds the largest coal reserves on earth, 27% of the world total.[17]

The US can also boast of large natural ports on both the Atlantic and the Pacific oceans, the longest network of navigable rivers in the world, as well as "gigantic arable landmasses."[18] The Mississippi, Missouri, Red, and Ohio rivers link the US breadbasket to the Gulf of Mexico, providing a natural transportation system capable of moving goods from the US to the global market cheaply and efficiently. The establishment of large land transportation networks, first through the railways and then through interstate highways, has further increased the capacity for the different manufacturing regions in the country to sell their goods between states as well as to provide inexpensive access to coastal regions for world trade.

The Not-so-Lucky

- **Africa:** For Canada and the US, size and an abundance of natural resources worked to their economic advantage. But even though Africa has both size and a wealth of natural resources, the continent remains one of the poorest in the world. How has this happened? One reason is that, unlike in Canada and the US, Africa's size doesn't work to its benefit. Where Canada and the US are single countries, Africa's total area is made up of some fifty smaller countries, each with its own political agenda, policies, and problems. According to Oxford economics professor Anthony J. Venebles, this "fragmentation into small countries with poor neighbors has been part of the problem underlying Africa's poor economic performance."[19]

    Geographically, communication between neighboring countries is often difficult, given that sub-Saharan Africa has "virtually no navigable rivers and few natural harbours."[20] Africa's landlocked nations have little access to international or world markets. Moreover, there is little high-quality agricultural space available, and because most of the continent receives very little rainfall, even quality agricultural land is constantly susceptible to draught. Both human and animal disease are also a constant worry; some economists have even suggested that malaria has had a significant impact on economic performance, inhibiting as much as 10% of GDP over the fifteen-year period between 1980 and 1995.[21]

Equally problematic is the fact that, in a continent made up of a great number of smaller political entities, "geographically concentrated natural endowments—such as mineral resources, coasts or rivers—are likely to be unevenly distributed, . . . meaning that . . . coordination failures are acute, and natural endowments are not used effectively."[22] An uneven distribution of resources has led some countries to concentrate almost exclusively on the single natural resource to which they have access, which leaves their economies vulnerable. Botswana, for instance, depends almost entirely on diamond mining; as a result, it was hit especially hard when a joint venture by the foreign-owned De Beers Corporation and the Botswana government temporarily suspended production in 2009 as consumer demand declined during the height of the global recession. Because diamond production constitutes 75% of Botswana's export earnings, the halt in production caused a massive 12% contraction of national GDP.[23]

The uneven distribution of resources across the continent further compounds high levels of religious, ethnic, and linguistic fragmentation. Nigeria provides one example; after the discovery of oil in Nigeria's southern delta during the 1970s, the country saw a massive influx of migrants from neighboring Ghana. Unfortunately, this triggered a xenophobic reaction within Nigeria, and "once economic conditions deteriorated, the Ghanaians were formally expelled" back to their home country, which was in the grip of a severe draught.[24] This soured relations between the two countries, choking off potential trade partnerships and resource export that could have improved both economies in the long term.

Nigeria's difficulties with managing its oil resources have continued in recent years. Like Botswana, Nigeria has become almost completely dependent on a single resource, oil, which, as of 2008, accounted for nearly 60% of the country's GDP.[25] As a result, Nigerians have mostly abandoned traditionally reliable agricultural commodities such as cocoa, rubber, and cotton. But increasing dependence on a single resource has also fomented the emergence of militant ethnic groups who, funded by corrupt and opportunistic local politicians, engaged in a vicious armed conflict with the government in an attempt to take control of the nation's oil reserves during the 1990s and early 2000s. As a result, the entire southern delta has become a militarized zone. Frequent attacks on foreign-owned pipelines and wells caused corporations such as Shell to cut oil production by more than a quarter, which had a predictably devastating effect on the Nigerian economy.[26]

Nigeria's oil troubles provide just one example of what economists have dubbed the "resource curse" afflicting several African countries. The resource curse refers to the paradoxical situation in which "economies with abundant natural resources have tended to grow less."[27] This is especially the case in countries like the Democratic Republic of Congo, Angola, Gabon, and, as already mentioned, Nigeria. Although naturally abundant in sought-after resources like cobalt, diamonds, copper, tin, and oil, these countries are also consistently among the worst performers in economic growth.[28] Along with poor resource management, lack of diversity, and political corruption, resource-rich countries tend to have a stronger currency, which impedes the trading of other exports. Perhaps most concerning is that many resource-rich African countries have not maintained anything close to sustainable growth strategies. These countries therefore fail to acknowledge "that if they do not reinvest their resource wealth into productive investments above the ground, they are actually becoming poorer."[29]

Any hope for improvement in Africa means overcoming the high degree of geographic and cultural fragmentation, as well as finding ways to diversify their economies so as to avoid over-dependence on a single natural resource. According to Joseph Stiglitz, this can be accomplished by building sustainable growth strategies through things "like training local workers, developing small- and medium-size enterprises to provide inputs for mining operations and oil and gas companies, domestic processing, and integrating the natural resources into the country's economic structure."[30] Yet this solution does not provide a means to overcome natural geographic barriers, such as impassable rivers or a lack of arable farmland. Because of such geographical barriers, many African countries may continue to struggle.

- **The Middle East:** Despite being one of the richest regions in the world in commodities like oil and gas, Middle Eastern countries like Iran, Iraq, Saudi Arabia, Qatar, Syria, Kuwait, the United Arab Emirates, and others struggle from geographical issues similar to many African countries. The Middle Eastern economy is almost entirely dominated by oil, which accounts for close to 30% of global crude production.[31] But the region's oil wealth is offset by the fact that it is one of the driest places in the world, and many parts of the region lack any permanent water bodies or perennial rivers whatsoever. Much of the Arabian peninsula (which includes Kuwait, Bahrain, Qatar, the United Arab Emirates, Oman, Yemen, and Saudi Arabia) is inhospitable, has virtually no arable farmland, forests, or mineral resources, and regularly suffers from low rainfall and water shortages. Moreover, farmers in ancient Mesopotamia (in what is today modern Iraq, northern Syria, and southeastern Turkey) had for centuries used seawater from the Persian Gulf to irrigate their fields, which ultimately made the soil in southern Iraq unusable, while areas with usable land for agriculture rely heavily on complex irrigation and desalination systems in order to sustain fragile, climate-sensitive agricultures.

Like many African countries, the Middle East's continued dependency on a single resource could spell trouble in the future. And though the Middle East won't run out of oil anytime soon, reliance on oil has led to a lack of economic diversification, while any fluctuations in the price of oil will have a severe impact on the entire region's economic health. Oil-producing countries have been propping up the Middle East financially, with workers from non oil-producing countries migrating to the oil producers to work. The income earned by these migrants is often sent back to their families, who then spend the money in their home nation. This income provides an economic boost for non-oil-producing countries, but also exacerbates dependency, so that the Middle East's entire economy stands or falls with the oil industry.

Given the volatility of oil as a commodity, the entire region finds itself in a rather precarious position, and further efforts must be made to develop alternative economic activities, whether in agriculture, the financial sector, or manufacturing. Local governments in the Middle East must create better tax incentives to attract innovative and diverse research and development to the region. Indeed, academics have found that local research and development can significantly increase the overall productivity of other economic activities in the vicinity.[32]

The Cost of Environmentalism Today

Economic policy decisions are deeply embedded within environmental, social, cultural, institutional, and political contexts. Hence, the ways in which western countries such as the US and Canada use their natural resources, and the subsequent effect of those uses on the environment, have come under close public scrutiny and protest in recent years. But wherever one stands on hotbed topics like the environment, I think most of us agree that we need to manage the planet's natural resources responsibly so that there's enough to go around for a long time. The risks involved in natural resource extraction, manufacture, importing, and exporting, have to be understood to ensure long-term benefits for our society and to prevent shortages that may lead to clashes over resources in the future. And because some of our most valuable resources (such as oil) are non-renewable, individuals, corporations, and governments need to carefully weigh the costs and benefits of activities and technologies that have a direct impact on the environment.

Conservation has long been part of the fabric of North American culture. Milestones over the centuries include the publication in 1854 of *Walden*, Henry David Thoreau's famous wilderness preservationist tract;

US president Theodore Roosevelt's creation of the Forestry Service; and the establishment of a swath of national parks and forest and wildlife preserves by both the US and Canadian governments in the mid-nineteenth and early twentieth centuries.[33] But the environmental movement as we know it today really took off during the cultural revolutions of the 1960s and 1970s. Those were the years when concerns about air and water pollution, energy shortages, and nuclear power came to the forefront of public consciousness after a series of high-profile ecological disasters, such as the contamination of a Japanese fishing boat from nuclear fallout in 1954 and the Santa Barbara oil spill in 1969. Anxieties about the environment crystallized with the creation of Earth Day in 1970, which was attended by an estimated twenty-million people in its first year. When the first full-view photograph of the earth from space was beamed down from Apollo 17 on December 7, 1972, the image seemed to encapsulate the environmental movement's anxieties about the fragility and beauty of the planet we call home, and the need to protect it from our own worst tendencies.

But even though it means well, today's environmental movement too often oversteps its bounds. In some cases, environmental activism devolves into something like a publicity stunt, with rich movie stars and musicians jumping at the chance to advocate causes with little understanding of the economic consequences for the broader public. When Paul McCartney and his then-wife Heather were sponsored by the US Humane Society to call for an end to the Canadian seal hunt in 2005, the pair were "the latest in a long list of celebrities . . . to publicly oppose the hunt" since the 1970s, when French actress Brigitte Bardot was photographed hugging seal pups on the Maritime ice floes.[34] In a statement to the Canadian Press the following year, McCartney remarked that the hunt "is something that leaves a stain on the character of the Canadian people and we don't think that's right. I don't think the vast amount of Canadians think that's right."[35]

Yet the McCartneys' assumptions about the seal hunt demonstrated a near-complete lack of understanding of the actual facts. Instead, they relied on peoples' emotional reactions to cute, furry baby seals and sensationalized rhetoric about cruelty and barbarism. In a televised debate with the McCartneys on CNN's Larry King Live, then-Newfoundland premier and Rhodes scholar Danny Williams set the record straight. Williams cited a quote from the World Wildlife Fund stating that the Canadian "sea harvest is conducted in a humane way, and . . . that the Canadian Harp seal hunt is professional, and highly regulated by comparison with seal hunts in Greenland and the north Atlantic. It has the potential to serve as a model to improve humane practice and reduce seal suffering with the other hunts." Williams proceeded to further debunk the idea that sealers are inhumane barbarians that "club" seals to death, a practice used in the past, but not today. Williams further commented that the seal herd had actually tripled since 1970, and that simply allowing the population to thrive unchecked would lead to far more inhumane consequences, such as the seals' starvation and the possible decimation of the local fish population, which would in turn adversely affect an already precarious fishing industry.[36]

Williams' real concern, however, was that the McCartneys were being used to further the propaganda of wealthy special interest groups like Greenpeace and People for the Ethical Treatment of Animals (PETA), when more credible scientific organizations like the International Society for Conservation, the World Wildlife Fund, and the International Fund for Animal Welfare had deemed the Canadian seal hunt humane.[37] As Williams caustically put it near the end of the debate: hugging baby seals makes for a good photo-op for wealthy celebrities who don't have to actually live and work in Atlantic Canada, but that's about it.

This is only one example of how the environmental movement has often used celebrities to further its cause and, as one sealer put it in a clip shown during the Williams–McCartney debate, allow special interest groups to "fill their coffers for another year."[38] In recent times, we've seen everyone from Meryl Streep condemning apple pesticides to former US vice-president Al Gore hawking DVDs about global warming. Yet celebrities who lend their personalities to a cause they don't fully understand can actually harm the very cause they claim to care so much about. Geology professor Ian Clark of the University of Ottawa has charged Gore's popular 2006 global-warming documentary *An Inconvenient Truth* with misrepresenting evidence about the correlation between carbon dioxide (CO_2) and rising climate temperatures. As Clark points out, "the rise in CO_2 lags the rise in temperature by about 800 years. This shows that CO_2 does not play a role in warming. . . . [Even w]hen the climate starts to cool, CO_2 remains high, again for hundreds of years, and so plays no role in sustaining the warm climate."[39] The problem is not that Gore wants to do his part to help the environment; rather, the problem is that the environmental movement's exploitation of celebrity culture, and vice versa, means that politicians, movie stars, and musicians start behaving as though they're experts in biology, economics, and geology. As Clark suggests, "Mr. Al Gore is a politician, and an opportunist who gains much from the business of global warming alarmism. *An Inconvenient Truth* is a pack of lies and misrepresentations. It has done much to damage science."[40]

Even scientists can be drawn into the agenda of the environmental movement, resulting in bias, partisanship, and groupthink that skew public opinion. Take the recent debate over the Alberta oil sands and the Keystone XL Pipeline, for instance. In 2008, Alberta-based TransCanada Corp. proposed a 3,461-kilometre pipeline system capable of delivering Canadian crude oil to refineries on the US Gulf coast. The pipeline was projected to inject roughly $1.7 trillion into the Canadian economy and $45 billion into the US economy over the next twenty-five years, along with creating up to half a million jobs by 2035.[41] The pipeline would also improve energy security by lessening US dependence on foreign oil reserves in unstable countries in the Middle East and South America, as well as boost the American economy by creating up to 20,000 well-paying construction and manufacturing jobs.[42] And with the global population projected to swell from seven to nine billion by 2050, energy demands will likely triple, while easily accessible crude is becoming more and more difficult to find.[43] Yet, using the overblown rhetoric typical of far too much environmental advocacy, NASA scientist James Hansen argued that developing the oil sands would be "game over" for the environment, since "Canada's tar sands . . . contain twice the amount of carbon dioxide emitted by global oil use in our entire history." Hansen paints a dire, apocalyptic picture: if we exploit the oil sands, we can expect that the "Western United States and the semi-arid region from North Dakota to Texas will develop semi-permanent drought, with rain, when it does come, occurring in extreme events with heavy flooding. . . . More and more of the Midwest would be a dust bowl. California's Central Valley could no longer be irrigated. Food prices would rise to unprecedented levels."[44] Coupled with mostly unfounded fears of groundwater contamination in Nebraska, the environmentalists' apocalyptic rhetoric won a temporary victory when President Obama decided to block development on the pipeline until after the November 2012 election.[45]

But it seems hyperbolic to suggest that the oil sands alone could wreak such extraordinary destruction on the environment and the economy.[46] For Clark, Hansen's rhetoric betrays advocacy rather than good science. "The oil sands," Clark writes, "contribute very, very little to global CO2. . . . The pollution and emissions from the oil sands have been greatly exaggerated. Killing the oil sands would be to the great detriment of all Canadians, from aboriginal groups to engineers and other workers alike. It is greener energy than many other sources."[47] Shutting down the oil sands does very little to help the environment, and much to damage both the US and Canadian economies in a time where job creation and a secure source of an important natural resource is desperately needed.

It's not a question of choosing economics over the environment or vice versa. Preserving natural resources and protecting endangered species are worthy causes, but targeting the oil sands seems to be a case of misplaced priorities. As Clark notes, "cutting off the oil sands energy supply will not reduce our addiction to fossil fuels. It will only require North Americans to import more."[48] Improved technologies have made oil extraction operations less environmentally disruptive and less polluting. Moreover, improving these technologies spurs innovation in a number of fields, from engineering to petroleum research, which not only drives economic development, but also pushes development in the direction of sustainable environmental practices. There are many serious environmental problems, such as human over-fishing, habitat destruction, and urban sprawl. All of these problems have far greater impact on the environment than the oil sands; it's to these concerns that the environmental movement should turn its attention. If the environmental movement doesn't get its priorities straight, it could end up making things worse, both economically and environmentally.

Destiny or Innovation?

Though Canada and the US have their share of economic, social, and political problems, it's fairly safe to say that living in either of these countries puts you at a significant economic and geographic advantage over those living in other parts of the world. Yes, Canada's winters are cold and, yes, the humidity in Florida can get pretty uncomfortable in July, but these are minor inconveniences next to, say, the sweltering, arid heat of an African desert, where a month or two of bad weather can lead to a potential famine that threatens the lives of millions of people.

Some geographic barriers may always exist and complicate the economic viability of certain regions of the globe. It's a fact that agricultural land remains scarce in hotter climates because the soil is too thin and hence the essential nutrients needed to sustain agricultural production are often blown away in dust storms or washed away by torrential rains.[49] No amount of free-flowing info-capital will ever *completely* overcome these kinds of concerns; regardless, in our increasingly globalized world, geographic barriers are less daunting than in the past. Both innovations in ICTs and improved distribution of these technologies could one day help reduce such barriers so that poorer countries might not only improve their own economic well-being, but also begin to actively contribute to and benefit from the world economy.

Key Takeaways

- Economic Geography studies the interrelationship between a region's geography and its economic practices, and the way that these practices are organized in space.

- Earlier theorists thought that global financial integration and the emergence of ICTs would ultimately bring about the end of geography. But the 2008 financial crisis suggested that geography still matters.

- Natural resources are not evenly distributed throughout the world; thus geography helps some regions flourish economically while it hinders others.

- Canada and the US are two nations with favourable economic geographies: both have an abundance of diverse natural resources, temperate climates, and easy access to world markets via large coastal regions, inland waterways, and transnational transportation networks.

- Despite being resource-rich, African and Middle Eastern economies have suffered from geographical disadvantages.

- Africa in particular suffers from a "resource curse," which describes a paradoxical situation in which resource-rich countries experience less growth than countries with fewer natural resources.

- Today's environmental movement must realign its priorities to meet with concrete, real-world issues, rather than use celebrities to push "fashionable" causes (Maritime seal hunt, Alberta oil sands, etc.).

- In the future, improved technology and distribution of technology may help mitigate geographical obstacles to economic development.

ENDNOTES

¹ Gunter Krumme, "Economic and Business Geography," 2002. <http://faculty.washington.edu/krumme/ecbusgeo.html>

² Richard O'Brien, *Global Financial Integration: The End of Geography* (Royal Institute of International Affairs, 1992).

³ Richard O'Brien and Alasdair Keith, "The Geography of Finance: After the Storm," *Cambridge Journal of Regions, Economy, and Society* (2009).

⁴ *Investopedia.com*, "When Wholesale Funding Goes Bad," 21 October 2009. <http://www.investopedia.com/articles/economics/09/when-wholesale-funding-goes-bad.asp#axzz2NXHRkCuT>

⁵ O'Brien and Keith, 2009.

⁶ John Kay qtd. in "Globalization," by Henry Wai-chung Yeung, *The Student's Companion to Geography* (Blackwell, 2002).

⁷ Statistics Canada, "Exports of Goods on Balance of Payments Basis, by Product," 2007–2012. <http://www.statcan.gc.ca/tables-tableaux/sum-som/l01/cst01/gblec04-eng.htm>

⁸ Howstuffworks.com, "Geography of Canada: Economy," N.d. <http://geography.howstuffworks.com/canada/geography-of-canada2.htm>

⁹ Ibid.

¹⁰ Ibid.

¹¹ *The Atlas of Canada*, "Energy," N.d. <http://atlas.nrcan.gc.ca/auth/english/maps/economic/energy/1>

¹² *Economy Watch*, "Canada Economy," 11 March 2010. <http://www.economywatch.com/world_economy/canada/?page=full>

¹³ US Central Intelligence Agency, "Canada," *CIA World Factbook*, 6 November 2012. <https://www.cia.gov/library/publications/the-world-factbook/geos/ca.html>

¹⁴ Revenue Watch, "How Is the Economic Crisis Changing the Management of Resource Wealth?" N.d. <http://www.revenuewatch.org/training/resource_center/backgrounders/how-economic-crisis-changing-management-resource-wealth>

¹⁵ Ibid.

16 Robert H. Weibe qtd. in "Historical Perspectives on US Economic Geography," by Sukkoo Kim and Robert A. Margo, National Bureau of Economic Research, Working Paper 9594, March 2003. <http://www.nber.org/papers/w9594.pdf?new_window=1>

17 US Central Intelligence Agency, "United States," *CIA World Factbook*, 6 November 2012. <https://www.cia.gov/library/publications/the-world-factbook/geos/us.html>

18 Bjorn Borgisky, "US Economic Geography," *Economy Watch*, 6 August 2009. <http://www.economywatch.com/economy-business-and-finance-news/US_Economic_Geography_08-06.html>

19 Anthony J. Venebles, "Economic Geography and African Development," 22 April 2010. <http://www.economics.ox.ac.uk/members/tvenables/images/stories/unpublishedpapers/pregsciafrica4.pdf>

20 Ibid.

21 Jeffrey Sachs and Pia Malaney, "The Economic and Social Burden of Malaria," *Nature*, No. 415, 7 February 2002.

22 Ibid.

23 Revenue Watch, N.d.

24 Venebles, 22 April 2012.

25 *Wikipedia*, "Conflict in the Niger Delta," N.d. <http://en.wikipedia.org/wiki/Conflict_in_the_Niger_Delta#The_Nigerian_oil_crisis>

26 BBC News, "Nigerian Government to Intervene in Oil Crisis," 10 October 1998. <http://news.bbc.co.uk/2/hi/africa/190594.stm>

27 Jeffrey Sachs and Andrew Warner, "Natural Resource Abundance and Economic Growth," NBER Working Paper No. 5398, December 1995. <http://www.nbcr.org/papers/w5398>

28 Elena Paltseva and Jesper Roine, "Are Natural Resources Good or Bad for Development?" Forum for Research on Eastern Europe and Emerging Economies, 21 November 2011. <http://freepolicybriefs.org/2011/11/21/are-natural-resources-good-or-bad-for-development/>

29 Joseph Stiglitz, "Africa's Natural Resources Can Be a Blessing, Not a Curse," *The Guardian*, 6 August 2012. <http://www.guardian.co.uk/business/economics-blog/2012/aug/06/africa-natural-resources-economic-curse>

[30] Ibid.

[31] Richard Cronin, "Natural Resources and the Development-Environment Dilemma," The Henry L. Stimson Centre, 2009. <http://www.stimson.org/images/uploads/research-pdfs/Exploiting_Natural_Resources-Chapter_5_Cronin.pdf>

[32] Sergey Lychagin, John Van Reenen, and Joris Pinkse, "You Can Raise Productivity Through R&D, but Geography Matters a Lot," Voxeu.org, 25 October 2010. <http://www.voxeu.org/article/location-location-location-why-geography-matters-rd>

[33] Monte Hummel, "Environmental and Conservation Movements," *The Canadian Encyclopedia*, N.d. <http://www.thecanadianencyclopedia.com/articles/environmental-and-conservation-movements>

[34] CBC News, "Harp Seal Hunt a 'Stain' on Canada, McCartney Says," 2 March 2006. <http://www.cbc.ca/news/canada/story/2006/03/02/mccartney-060302.html>

[35] Ibid.

[36] CNN, "Larry King Live [Transcript]," 3 March 2006. <http://transcripts.cnn.com/TRANSCRIPTS/0603/03/lkl.01.html>

[37] Ibid.

[38] Ibid.

[39] Yadullah Hussein, "The Environmental Movement Has Lost Its Way," *Financial Post*, 9 February 2012. <http://business.financialpost.com/2012/02/09/the-environmental-movement-has-lost-its-way/>

[40] Ibid.

[41] John H. Richardson, "Keystone," *Esquire*, 10 August 2012. <http://www.esquire.com/features/keystone-0912>

[42] *Washington Post*, "Keystone XL Pipeline Is the Wrong Target for Protesters" (Editorial), 10 October 2011. <http://www.washingtonpost.com/opinions/keystone-xl-pipeline-is-the-wrong-target-for-protesters/2011/10/07/gIQA4se6aL_story.html>

[43] Ibid.

[44] James Hansen, "Game Over for the Climate," *New York Times*, 9 May 2012. <http://www.nytimes.com/2012/05/10/opinion/game-over-for-the-climate.html?_r=0>

[45] John M. Broder, "US Delays Decision on Pipeline until After Election," *New York Times*, 10 November 2011. <http://www.nytimes.com/2011/11/11/us/politics/administration-to-delay-pipeline-decision-past-12-election.html>

[46] Ibid.

[47] Hussein, 9 February 2012.

[48] Ibid.

[49] Daron Acemoglu and James A. Robinson, "No, A Nation's Geography Is Not Its Destiny," Reuters, 19 March 2012. <http://blogs.reuters.com/great-debate/2012/03/19/no-a-nations-geography-is-not-its-destiny/>

Chapter Four

THE GOVERNMENT, THE ECONOMY, AND THE PUBLIC GOOD

"The government solution to a problem is usually as bad as the problem." – Milton Friedman

WHAT ROLE DOES government play in today's global financial picture? How do the decisions and policies of governments at home and abroad affect your personal or business finances? Over the course of this chapter, we will discuss a number of connected issues to address these questions, including the response by North American governments to the 2008 financial crisis, bailouts, the debate over austerity versus stimulus measures, federal tax and monetary policy, social policy, and how government bureaucracy and corruption retard economic growth.

The discussion provided here will give you a better understanding of the issues facing governments in today's global economy, but this is only a stepping stone. When it comes to governmental policy, even the most skeptical individual can be lulled into a false sense of security by thinking that, at the end of the day, governments are looking out for the public good. This is not always the case. Ultimately, it is up to you, and you alone, to look after your own best interests. Doing so will help you regain some measure of control over your finances, even in the face of questionable decisions by governments.

Response to the Financial Crisis of 2008

Governments and politicians often seem far more concerned with making policy choices that will get them elected or re-elected. And not unlike labor unions, governments today have failed to properly grasp the limits of their powers in the face of the 2008 financial crisis and subsequent recession. We can see clear examples of this kind of fiscal and political gerrymandering in the way that North American governments responded to this crisis. Let's briefly recap the conditions that governments were forced to address when the financial crisis hit in 2008:

- Over 25 banks worldwide were on the brink of failure.
- The global stock market was in a free-fall.
- The IMF predicted a worldwide recession of -0.3 GDP for 2009.[1]

What caused these conditions to occur? Why haven't we recovered from them yet? And why don't things seem to be improving? There is rarely a single right answer to these kinds of questions, writes Stanford professor of economics John B. Taylor, but the research "strongly suggests that specific government actions and interventions should be first on the list of answers to all three."[2] Likewise, Warren Buffet's annual letter to stakeholders in 2011 suggested that everyone—"government, lenders, borrowers, the media, rating agencies, you name it"—was guilty of the "destructive behavior" that led to the crisis.[3] Is it a coincidence that smart guys like Taylor and Buffet place government first on the list of economic offenders? Let's look at some of the reasons why they might have put them there.

Bailouts

When the US housing bubble burst in late 2007 and markets around the world began to fall, many governments resorted to bailouts to stave off financial disaster. By September 2009, government use of massive taxpayer-funded stimulus packages amounted to almost $11 trillion.[4] But throwing still more capital into a broken system is only a short-term solution: it's a band-aid for a gunshot wound.

One of the first questions to ask is why governments see bailouts as a viable option in times of economic crisis. Why would governments hand over taxpayer money to help out unsuccessful financial firms? When governments provide a bailout they are, in fact, following a well-established principle of economic policy. In his classic 1873 study *Lombard Street: A Description of the Money Market*, British businessman Walter Bagehot emphasized that the most important thing for the central bank to do is to prevent panic in times of crisis, and it does that by giving the impression that everything's fine: "what is necessary to stop a panic is to diffuse the impression, that though money may be dear, still money is to be had. . . . [The central bank ought to] lend freely, boldly, and so that the public may feel [they] mean to go on lending."[5] In other words, continued spending and lending maintains confidence in the financial and banking systems, preventing a panic that would throw the markets into chaos.

We can see this policy at work in the US government's response to the fallout from the collapse of investment bank Bear Stearns in 2008 and, later that same year, Fannie Mae and Freddie Mac. In the wake of the subprime mortgage crisis, Bear Stearns became the subject of rumors that it would soon fail; and "rumors," as Bagehot knew and former Bear Stearns CEO Alan Greenberg told Frontline, "are such that they can just plain put you out of business."[6] Burdened by billions of dollars of bad mortgages, Bear Stearns' stock had dropped from $172 to $57 a share, and the company found itself mere hours from bankruptcy. Federal Reserve Chairman Ben Bernanke took action. To stabilize the markets, Bernanke engineered a marriage between Bear Sterns and the commercial bank J. P. Morgan Chase & Co., with a promise that the Federal Reserve would provide a $30-billion loan to cover Bear Stearns' questionable assets tied to toxic mortgages. It was an unprecedented effort by a government agency to stop the contagion of fear threatening the rest of Wall Street.

The Fed's decision to bankroll a merger between Bear Stearns and J. P. Morgan gave way to the largest financial-rescue plan in US history. In September 2008, the US Treasury placed Fannie Mae and Freddie Mac in conservatorship to keep them solvent, but then investment bank giant Lehmann Brothers claimed bankruptcy under massive real estate debts. A day later, American International Group (AIG)—the largest insurance company in the world—also collapsed. As with the Bear Stearns collapse, it seemed that the government had no choice but to step in. Unwilling and unable to manage the burden, banks would no longer make loans to companies or to each other. So the federal government tried to promote confidence in the economy by purchasing the troubled assets hindering the financial system. The government threw taxpayer money at the problem to remediate Wall Street's bad deals.

On October 3, 2008, the US congress passed the $700-billion Emergency Economic Stabilization Act. The bill authorized the US Treasury to buy high-risk and non-performing debt, which included mortgages, auto loans, and college loans from several lending institutions.[7] All banks, whether they were struggling or not, were forced to accept $250 billion of the $700 billion bailout to protect the identity of those banks at risk of collapsing. A month later, General Motors and Chrysler received almost $100 billion in bailout funds. Even though the automakers' trouble was not directly related to Wall Street, the government kept doling out cash under the pretense of saving the economy. This began what I like to call the bailout fad. Bailouts caught on with governments around the world: Germany, Italy, South Korea, Great Britain, and, of course, Greece, engineered stimulus packages to protect their banks.

Although lauded for regulating one of the safest banking systems in the world, the Canadian government also fell victim to the bailout fad. An April 2013 report by the Canadian Centre for Policy Alternatives (CCPA) showed that Canadian banks received close to $114 billion from government agencies during the 2008 crisis. According to CCPA senior economist David MacDonald, "'three of Canada's banks—CIBC,

BMO, and Scotiabank—were completely under water, with government support exceeding the market value of the company'."[8] So "safe" in this instance simply meant that the Canadian government did a better job at hiding how bad things actually were. What's worse, the CCPA's analysis found that Canadian lenders double-dipped, receiving funds from the bailout program set up by the US Federal Reserve as well as $41 billion from the Bank of Canada.[9] The government, naturally, denies calling it a bailout, but what else do you call handing over the equivalent of nearly 7% of Canada's GDP to struggling banks?[10] Even more troubling is the fact that the Canadian government kept most of this information from the public, playing a cynical political game of out of sight, out of mind.

Deficit Reduction: Austerity or Stimulus?

Billions of dollars have been thrown at banks to keep them afloat while taxpayers suffer. Bank bailouts have contributed to a huge national debt and forced governments to decide whether to spend on job creation programs, thereby adding to the debt, or promote austerity in an effort to encourage confidence from businesses and consumers alike. Though there have been modest gains in countries like Ireland, so far austerity has mostly been a failure. One need only look back to Greece to see the results. Although the Greek economy has shown some moderate gains with austerity measures, the Greeks themselves don't seem to be feeling any more confident about their prospects. Despite bailouts of hundreds of billions of euros, Greek leaders have admitted to facing huge shortfalls because tax revenue and other sources of potential income have become even scarcer. The recession and budget cuts have left businesses and individuals with less money to pay to taxes, and given them a greater incentive to avoid paying amounts owed. With less cash on hand, consumers have limited their spending; as a result, thousands of taxpaying businesses have failed. Additional income that was expected from a higher, 23% value-added tax required by the Greek bailout agreement fell short by around $800 million euros in the first four months of 2012, in part because cash-strapped businesses that used to be law-abiding have taken to hiding money just to remain in business.

The question now is whether governments should be spending more to improve the economy, or saving to reduce federal deficits. It's a tough call: spending is needed, but deficits will only increase national debt. Current examples of austerity measures haven't proved to be too kind or too effective. The PIIGS countries each adopted harsh austerity policies and in all of them unemployment rates have risen. Reductions in budget deficits also weren't as expected, given that tax receipts fell as output and employment suffered. The GDP seems to be getting worse rather than better. Austerity economists insisted that, in spite of high unemployment rates, cutting government spending would encourage confidence and lead to increased consumer and business spending. But, in the end, the economic and psychologically depressing effects of austerity actually saw a fall in private spending, as people didn't trust that their money would be safe in the market.

So austerity doesn't appear to be the answer. What about stimulus plans? There too, there is scant evidence of success. In the US, President Obama created a monumental stimulus package to get the economy back on track. On February 17, 2009, Obama signed the $797-billion American Recovery and Reinvestment Act (ARRA) into law. Paired with former president George W. Bush's stimulus package of a few months prior, Obama's new bill funneled nearly $1 trillion into the US economy. The breadth of the ARRA package was enormous, covering roads, education, airports, unemployment, and other benefits. However, a great deal of money was wasted on unnecessary projects. In the summer of 2010, US senators John McCain (R-AZ) and Tom Coburn (R-OK) released a report listing some questionable funding decisions. These included spending over $550,000 to replace the windows on a closed Visitor's Centre in Washington State and $1.2 million to turn an abandoned New Jersey train station into a museum. Even funds that were put to good use aren't having a lasting impact.[11] The US has since suffered a record low in unemployment while the government only added to its already massive debt.

Canada too fell victim to the stimulus "bug." In 2008, the minority Conservative government released a fiscal plan that balked at introducing new spending measures. Instead, the minority government would "rely on past tax reductions and infrastructure spending programs" to mitigate economic slowdown.[12] However, the left-leaning opposition Liberal and National Democratic parties formed a coalition and threatened to defeat the government unless it implemented an aggressive stimulus package. Hence, in January 2009, the Canadian government found themselves passing the over-ambitious Economic Action Plan. The Plan was to serve as a short-term stimulus package designed to "create jobs, build infrastructure, accelerate housing construction, stimulate spending by Canadians, and support businesses and communities."[13] The stimulus itself came with a hefty $34 billion price tag and the promise of "five years of red ink," after which the government expected a modest $700 million surplus.[14] But current research suggests that the impact of the stimulus has been minimal. According to the Simon Fraser Institute, a Canadian free-market think tank, "government spending and infrastructure investment accounted for just 0.2 percentage points of the 1.1 per cent growth between the second and third quarters of 2009."[15] What's worse, Canada's debt has swelled $124 billion between 2007–2008 and 2012, pushing back the government's long-term goal of erasing public debt from 2021 to 2042.[16] Rather than balance the books, as the minority Conservatives had originally intended, political pressure forced the Canadian government to spend money they didn't have on programs that haven't worked.

In short: both austerity and stimulus don't really seem to work, and both will have us paying for our mistakes well into the future. Ultimately, as John Maynard Keynes declared seventy-five years ago, "'the boom, not the slump, is the right time for austerity'."[17] Slashing spending while the economy is deeply depressed will only make things worse. Consumer spending makes up roughly 70% of the US economy, so in order for the country to do well, the government is counting on still more consumer spending. But with unemployment hovering around 9%, and many more people working but underemployed, Americans don't have a lot of extra spending money. At the same time, lack of funds has caused a dramatic shift in people's approach to spending. When the market was charting upwards, credit became widely used to support a lifestyle beyond the means of most families. There was a sense that people deserved to spend more on far more frivolous items, from the latest cell phone to the biggest entertainment system to overpriced handbags. A kind of toxic attitude had consumers feeling that they'd earned these luxury items. But the recession was very sobering, and has had a significant impact on this kind of spending.

The Road to Recovery

Given all these concerns, it's clear that monetary reform needs to be a priority for North American governments. But any effort to repay debt is going to hurt. Just cutting spending while failing to increase revenues might prove to be a disastrous decision. Again, when economic strength is so closely related to spending, it's important to help the middle-class prosper.

And yet, in October of 2011, a $447-billion jobs plan stalled in the US Senate.[18] The rejected package included an extension and expansion of the current payroll tax cut, an extension of jobless benefits to help the unemployed, new tax credits for businesses that hire the long-term unemployed, and additional funds to help save and create jobs for teachers and first responders such as firefighters. In other words, measures that aimed to provide some stability for the middle-class. Luckily, the payroll tax cut was later extended but, despite the obvious need, it was a challenge to get people on the same side. One of the reasons for this was the inclusion of a surtax on annual incomes over $1 million, a provision that Republicans strongly opposed. As I have already discussed, and will address in more detail in the "Tax Policy" section that follows, such tax-the-rich measures are deeply misguided.

Not only did the inclusion of such a measure forestall the jobs plan by creating a partisan schism on the Senate floor, but, by levying tax penalties against the country's job creators, it would also counteract the very measures within the plan that were designed to create jobs.

The bottom line is that neither stimulus nor deficit reduction alone will do the necessary work to pull governments out of an economic tailspin. And there's no simple answer: aspects of both are necessary. As part of the push for austerity in the US, mandatory sequester, an automatic reduction in spending that was set to begin in 2013, requires a $1.2-trillion cut over the next ten years, equaling a decrease of roughly $110 billion a year.[19] Approximately half of the cuts will come from the discretionary budget, including a 2% reduction in Medicare reimbursement. On the other hand, Washington raised the debt ceiling in January 2012 with far less hoopla than in the summer of 2011. In Canada, the government's 2012 budget was explicitly designed to implement belt-tightening austerity measures after short-term stimulus spending by scaling back retirement benefits, restricting immigration quotas to compensate for skills shortages, and expanding Canada's free-trade agreements. Like the US budget, Canadian austerity measures have set a three-year plan that hopes to slash spending by $5.2 billion in 2015.[20]

As a balance to austerity measures, governments should spend on long-term investments that earn a return like roads and dams, medical research, and education. If we want to see government money put to good use, it should go into investing in human capital, producing highly trained manpower for high-end, value-added services such as scientific and engineering expertise.

Tax Policy

Another important factor in the way that the US government has mismanaged its response to the global financial crisis is by creating and enforcing tax policies designed to generate political, rather than economic, benefits. But the most popular tax policies aren't necessarily the right ones, and following the will of a populace that doesn't even understand basic financial concepts will create far more problems than solutions when it comes to taxation.

The most popular rhetoric concerning taxes in today's political climate focuses on taxing the rich. Raising taxes for the "1%" made headline news throughout much of 2011 and 2012, especially when Warren Buffet suggested in a 2011 op-ed for the *New York Times* that the super-rich should be taxed at a higher rate. He pointed to the inequity in the percentage of income people at different tax levels pay in taxes, saying that, although his previous federal tax bill was $6,938,744, the large sum only amounted to 17.4% of his taxable income—a lower percentage than was paid by his employees whose "tax burdens ranged from 33 percent to 41 percent and averaged 36 percent."[21] President Obama endorsed Buffet's comment and used it to attack the Republicans: "I put a deal before the Speaker of the House, John Boehner, that would have solved this problem," Obama stated. Yet, "he walked away because his belief was we can't ask anything of millionaires and billionaires and big corporations in order to close our deficit."[22]

Given the split between the Republican House and the Democratic Senate, US lawmakers were then forced to spend the entire summer of 2011 engaged in a partisan battle over spending and taxes when addressing the need to raise the country's debt ceiling. The fight raged on for more than three months before an agreement was reached on August 2 to raise the $14.3-trillion US debt ceiling to avoid default. The agreement required at least $2.4 trillion in spending cuts over ten years, $900 billion of which would be seen in across-the-board cuts immediately. So there would be severe cuts, but no increase in revenues. This meant future government spending would be reduced at a time when recovery had stalled, the economy was fragile, unemployment rates remained high, and job creation was virtually nil.

The revenue problem, it seems, falls squarely on the shoulders of the wealthy. With the tax cuts ordered by George W. Bush expiring in January 2013, the second-term Obama administration has proposed raising the income tax on top US earners from 35% to 39.6%, while also tabling a proposal to increase tax rates on capital gains and dividends.[23] But there are significant problems with this approach:

- **High Taxes Create Disincentives:** High taxes for the wealthy create disincentives for economic growth. We've already seen the example of Facebook co-founder Eduardo Saverin, who renounced his US citizenship when faced with the prospect of higher taxes on his $3-billion fortune. As a result, Saverin's entrepreneurial savvy, along with his considerable capital, will seek opportunities in more willing markets, further starving the hungry maw of the US economy. The optics of Saverin's decision are absolutely terrible: his defection sends a message to businesspeople around the world that, in the US, politics take precedence over sound economic policy, and, as a result, the US may no longer be seen as the best place for wealthy companies or individuals to invest and grow their businesses.

- **Higher Taxes ≠ Higher Revenue:** Here's a shocking fact: historically, higher tax rates almost never generate higher revenue. According to political economist Dennis J. Mitchell, "[t]here is a distinct pattern throughout American history: When tax rates are reduced, the economy's growth rate improves and living standards increase. . . . Conversely, periods of higher tax rates are associated with sub-par economic performance and stagnant tax revenues."[24] Mitchell frames the issue by looking at how former US presidents John F. Kennedy and Ronald Reagan generated significant amounts of revenue by cutting taxes. For Kennedy, the result of cutting taxes was a 62% jump in tax revenues between 1961 and 1968, while Reagan's tax cuts during the 1980s saw total tax revenues increase even more dramatically, to 99.4%.[25] The reason is simple and goes back to my earlier point about disincentives: at some point, higher taxes actively discourage economic activities that will be taxed. As fiscal policy expert J. D. Foster writes, those who are subject to the higher tax rates always adjust their behavior: they'll take "fewer business risks, work fewer hours (or even retire), and save less."[26] When it comes to taxation, the law of inverse proportions holds sway: high taxes mean low productivity and low growth, while lower taxes means higher productivity and higher economic growth.

- **The Rich Contribute *More* when Taxed *Less*:** Yet another surprising fact: if you really want to soak the rich, keep taxes low. We can again look to the historical examples of Kennedy and Reagan. During Kennedy's presidency, tax revenue "from those making over $50,000 per year climbed by 57 percent between 1963 and 1966." This meant that the rich actually "saw their portion of the income tax burden" rise from 11.6% to 15.1%. During the Reagan years (1981–1988), the share of income tax revenue paid by the top 10% of earners went from 48% to 57.2%.[27] This demonstrates that "the best way to entice the rich to pay even more tax is to keep rates low and allow them to get even richer."[28] Moreover, the idea that the rich aren't paying their fair share is a complete fabrication. In Britain, for instance, recent statistics suggest that the top earners are paying far more in taxes than their share of the total income. The top 1% of British earners, those who make £156,000 or higher per year (approximately $250,000 US) will pay 24% of all income tax collected for the 2012 fiscal year, while the top 10% (those making at least £50,500 per year) will pay a whopping 55%. Wealthy Brits are already contributing almost 80% of the total tax revenue, with the wealthiest paying roughly 14% more in taxes than their actual share of total income.[29]

- **Taxing the Rich Won't Actually Pay the Bills:** In reality, US federal taxes would have to be doubled for all tax brackets to close the debt-financing gap. According to the website USdebtclock.org, the total US debt surpassed $56 trillion, or $180,000 for every US citizen, at the beginning of 2012. Another sobering look at the US' liabilities was shown in *I.O.USA*, a 2008 American documentary film directed by Patrick Creadon.

According to the film, the US would have to raise federal taxes across the board twofold to make up for its deficits. Of course, the budget approved by the Obama administration claims that raising taxes on the top 2% of income earners will generate $836.5 billion over the next ten years: that's exactly what people want to hear. The only problem is that this projection ignores the actual harm that this policy will do the economy as a whole over that same time period. Even if we accept the revenue estimates, along with the proposed spending cuts in the Obama administration's budget, the federal debt held by the public will rise by $8.5 trillion in the same time period without the tax hike, and by $7.7 trillion with the tax hike. In short, "allowing some of the Bush tax cuts to expire as Obama demands represents less than 10 percent of the projected debt increase."[30] Conversely, a recent study by Ernst and Young suggests that Obama's tax policy could result in a $200 billion fall in long-term economic output, a loss of 710,000 jobs, a drop in wages, and an overall drop in standard of living for the American lower- and middle-class, the very audience to whom Obama's tax hike appeals.[31]

Given these facts, it's increasingly hard to see how taxing the rich can function as anything more than political sloganeering. It provides the lower- and middle-classes with an easy scapegoat that allows them to turn the focus away from the hard questions they should be asking themselves about their own economic behavior and, worst of all, keeps them ignorant about the facts themselves. Equally damaging, however, is the fact that this kind of policy misrepresents the actual problem: hyper-complicated tax codes with all kinds of loopholes that allow a minority of wealthy corporations to avoid shouldering their fair share of the tax burden. It is common practice for politicians to bribe voters with entitlements come election time, and increasingly we are seeing how a certain minority of the super-rich has politicians under their control.

We can see an example of this when we look at how a few wealthy companies have exploited the government's corporate tax policies. On the one hand, it would seem that corporations pay too much tax: at 35%, the US has the second highest corporate tax rate in the world. What's more, the US is one of the only countries to tax its multinationals on their foreign earnings. Hence, corporate executives and CEO's persistently lobby the US Congress to lower the corporate tax rate so that their companies can remain competitive. The problem is that, unlike most other countries, the US corporate tax rate is riddled with loopholes, special tax breaks, and shelters that allow certain corporations to pay far less. At the end of the day, some US corporations actually "pay only slightly more on average than their counterparts in other industrial countries. And some American corporations use aggressive strategies to pay less—often far less—than their competitors abroad and at home."[32] In such an uneven tax system, genuine innovation takes a backseat to "creative" (re: disingenuous) bookkeeping practices, which end up costing the federal government even more in lost revenue. As one critic puts it, the corporate tax code has essentially allowed some US multinationals to become "'world leaders in tax avoidance'."[33]

Certainly, governments ought to continue to close these loopholes and come down hard on those companies that exploit the tax code or use their influence over government officials to create unfair advantages. But part of the reason that these loopholes exist in the first place is because of unscrupulous politicians bowing to corporate interests who then provide these politicians with the money to buy their votes. The fact is that the corporations themselves don't have the power to actually change the tax code: that responsibility falls entirely on the government. So it isn't the corporations that we should blame so much as weak politicians who are looking out for their own best interests rather than those of their constituents.

Social Policy

Another important issue facing governments today, especially in the face of the global recession that followed the financial crisis of 2008, is the question of how to reshape social policies. With debts continuing to rise, governments are finding themselves without the capital to pay for social programs. By throwing money into ineffective short-term solutions like stimulus plans, governments have essentially mortgaged the future of their citizens by making it extremely difficult to cover the costs of entitlement programs such as social security, heath care, welfare, and other social-safety-net benefits that provide aid to individuals and families facing hardship (the refundable portion of the earned-income; Supplemental Security Income for the elderly or disabled in the US; Old Age Security in Canada; unemployment insurance; as well as various assistance programs like food stamps, school meals, low-income housing assistance, and child-care assistance). And because of the housing bubble, wage and hiring freezes, and job loss from outsourcing and automation, many more people are finding themselves in the unenviable position of having to rely on entitlement programs to meet basic needs.

One of the more pressing concerns is the aging global population. According to US economist Edward Yardeni, our "'dismal demographic scenario is that the number of older people will grow faster than younger ones almost everywhere in the world'."[34] A recent estimate by the United Nations corroborates Yardeni's "'dismal'" scenario: in over seventy countries, birth rates have fallen to the point where they no longer meet replacement levels, while the high standard of living in developed countries means that even larger numbers of people are living longer.[35] One of the consequences is that the dependency ratio—which shows the number of people over the age of sixty-five, compared with those younger than sixty-five—will rise from about 20% to 40% in the next two decades.[36] This puts enormous pressure on governments to meet increasing monetary demands for social programs like health care/Medicare, Old Age Security (OAS), and government pensions like the Canada Pension Plan (CPP). We can see here globalization's ripple effect working on a governmental scale: governments' decisions to continue spending via taxpayer-funded bailouts and stimulus packages have effectively undermined these same governments' capacity to save enough capital for the increased costs of future entitlements.

At the same time, governments also seem to have had extraordinary difficulties in balancing the need for social programs with fiscal responsibility. For example, despite having very little money to actually pay for future entitlements, recent data suggests that the US government is still spending more than ever on social programs. As Nicholas Eberstadt of the American Enterprise Institute points out, in recent years US federal social policy has transformed the government into "an entitlements machine": "As a day-to-day operation, [the federal government] devotes more attention and resources to the public transfer of money, goods and services to individual citizens than to any other objective, spending more than for all other ends combined."[37] As the chart below demonstrates, the US government's expenditures on entitlement programs over the last fifty years have soared to just about two-thirds of all federal spending.

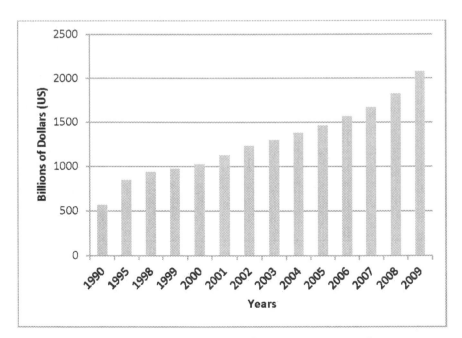

Figure 4–1: A summary of government transfer payments to individuals, 1990–2009[38]

Eberstadt points to another troubling fact: despite their reputations, the famously fiscally tight-fisted and anti-big-government Republicans have been spending just as much, if not more, than their traditionally free-spending Democratic counterparts. He says that "irrespective of the reputations and the rhetoric of the Democratic and Republican parties today, the . . . correspondence between Republican presidencies and turbocharged entitlement expenditures should underscore the unsettling truth that both political parties have, on the whole, been working together in an often unspoken consensus to fuel the explosion of entitlement spending."[39] The unsettling truth is that the *only two viable political options* that US citizens can vote for are equally irresponsible when it comes to spending on social programs.

We can see a further example of bad social policy in the US government's distribution of the money they do spend on entitlements. The US has been running huge annual surpluses in social security programs for years. That means that not as much is being spent as planned, so the extra money can be used elsewhere. With soon-to-be retiring baby boomers eligible for Medicare and social security benefits, however, social security programs will be paying out more than they collect in a few years. Rather than helping reduce the federal deficit, social security will actually be adding to it.

And there is some debate about whether social security for retirees is being abused. Though the entitlement system works to redistribute wealth, funds aren't redistributed from rich to poor but from young to old, from middle-class families to retirees. In 2009, the net worth of households headed by senior citizens was forty-seven times the net worth of those headed by people under thirty-five.[40] Yet seniors naturally vote to protect programs that distribute to the old and away from the young. The Congressional Budget Office's latest report on income inequality notes that growing Medicare costs partly explain why upper-income retirees receive a larger share of federal spending than they did thirty years ago, while working-age households with children receive "a much smaller and declining share of transfers."[41] Future generations will not enjoy the same quality of life as their elders because the government hasn't gotten the balance right. "The equalizing effect of federal taxes was smaller" in 2007 than in 1979, as "the composition of federal revenues shifted away from progressive income taxes to less-progressive payroll taxes," the budget office has said.[42] And federal benefit payments are doing less to even out the distribution of income. A growing share of benefits, like social security, goes to older Americans no matter what their income, so those who are working age end up paying for retirees.

As for Canada, it wasn't hit as hard by the economic recession as the US, and so the situation in the former is not quite as troubling as it is in the latter. One of the reasons that programs like the CPP have been able to stay above water is that ever since the mid-1990s, a growing number of people past the age of fifty-five find themselves still working to maintain their standard of living. "Freedom fifty-five" is yet another fairy tale sold to us by insurance companies and corporations that can create unrealistic expectations, feelings of entitlement, and, if it doesn't come true, resentment. The numbers are clear: on average, Canadians have *never* achieved freedom at fifty-five. Between 1976 and 2000, the average Canadian's retirement age fell from 65 to an all-time low of 61.5. In the past decade, however, the number hasn't dropped, and it's not likely to do so in the near future.[43]

It's true that the growing trend of people working past fifty-five may help the CPP stay financially viable in the future, but it also means that people will simply have to expect that they will be working well beyond fifty-five. Regardless of whether the CPP stays viable, we should remain ever vigilant about saving for our retirements. We should not, and cannot, expect the government to take care of us when we're old. Old Age Security and the CPP don't even come close to providing the necessary income for a comfortable retirement.

Bureaucracy and Corruption

So far we've been looking almost exclusively at the different problems that North American governments are facing today as a result of the financial crisis. This section shifts gears to explore two broader trends in government that threaten economic and social stability: out-of-control bureaucracies and the threat of corruption. In the current economic climate, governments face the difficult task of reducing the size of an overstaffed public sector to increase economic growth and cut deficits. This is proving difficult, however, because of entrenched government bureaucrats who enjoy lifetime entitlements, overly generous pension plans, and ample opportunity to abuse their authority.

Research shows that countries with large public sectors have generally lower economic growth (See Figure 4–2). This is especially the case in Europe, where governments are larger and spend on average 10% more of GDP than non-European governments. Much of this increased spending is the by-product of the size of government. A World Bank report showed that, in 2010, Western European countries spent 9% more of GDP than Canada, the US, Australia, and Japan. During the 2000s, Western European countries also spent more on their public sectors than Eastern European countries, and had larger governments by about 7% of GDP. In the same study, the World Bank also found that, in Europe, a "10 percentage-point increase in initial government size leads to a reduction in annual growth by 0.6–0.9 percentage points."[44]

Why do large bureaucracies hinder economic growth? One reason is that a large public sector can crowd out employment in the private sector, stifling innovation to protect the status quo. Entrenched bureaucracies also tend to increase dependency on public wages and benefits, and the larger the group of people that depend on the public sector to provide these benefits, the stronger the political demand for public programs that put even more strain on taxes and government spending.[45] Large government bureaucracies also mean that too much time and effort goes into paper shuffling and red tape, which hinders efficiency and works to the benefit of politicians rather than the governed. Politicians have used bureaucratic tactics like obstructionism to gain political leverage even while people suffer from the governments' inability to make timely decisions. More troubling, however, is that countries with a large public sector often give rise to an array of special interest groups far more interested in exploiting power and influence for their own benefit rather than growing the economy. This can also give rise to political corruption, which invariably leads to bad economic policy.

The World Bank declared corruption to be "'the single greatest obstacle to economic and social development'," and it estimates that more than $1 trillion (US) in bribes are handed out each year.[46] Of particular concern is the corruption that occurs within government institutions themselves. Politicians, public officials, and legislators hold bureaucratic positions that grant them both power and influence. When bureaucrats abuse their power, they can significantly harm economic and social development. And corruption at one level of government is often aided and abetted by dishonest behavior elsewhere. Corruption in the public sector is therefore often considered especially dangerous, since it seems to be at once everywhere and nowhere, all pervasive and yet difficult to root out.

To properly grasp the causes and consequences of corruption, we need to understand what economists call "rent-seeking" behavior. What an economist means by "rent" is rather different from what most people normally understand by the term. "Economic rent," according to IMF economist Paolo Mauro, can be defined as "the extra amount paid . . . to somebody or for something useful whose supply is limited either by nature or through human ingenuity."[47] Take Canadian hockey star Sidney Crosby, for example. Crosby possesses a rare natural talent for scoring a lot of goals in the best hockey league in the world and, over the next five years, he's being paid upwards of $62.5 million US to use that particular gift.[48] If Mr. Crosby did not possess such talent, however, his income would likely be significantly less, say $40,000 a year (x5 years = $200,000). This $62.3 million difference is the economic rent accruing to Mr. Crosby because individuals with his natural talent are in (very) short supply.

So it goes for natural limitations of supply, but what about artificial limitations? Mauro cites the example of the US government restricting imports of Japanese cars during the 1980s. This created an artificial shortage of Japanese-made cars in the US, which allowed American car companies like GM to both sell more vehicles and raise their prices, thereby accruing an economic rent on the difference between the price of domestic cars and the cheaper, but unavailable, Japanese cars. Japanese automakers also acquired economic rent from the US government's restriction on imports, since the demand for their product exceeded an artificially low supply. So where might the problem arise? Although not all rent-seeking behavior is illegal, it definitely has a corrupting influence on people in power. Private companies spend vast amounts of resources to convince governments to artificially restrict competition so that some company or individual can take advantage of economic rent. As a result, government bureaucrats across the globe are constantly "maneuvering to position themselves in a tiny monopoly where they can be bribed for issuing a license, approving an expenditure, or allowing a shipment across a border."[49] Hence, wherever bureaucrats have the most influence and discretion in applying government regulations, individuals are willing to bribe public officials to cut through any red tape. Sadly, officials are often willing to take these bribes.

What sorts of government policy tend to encourage corruption via rent-seeking behavior? Mauro identifies several:

- **Trade Restriction:** Government-induced restrictions on trade often promote rent seeking; by creating artificial limitations on foreign imports, import licenses become hot commodities. Hence, importers will be given the incentive to bribe officials to obtain these licenses. At the same time, trade restrictions can also create artificial monopolies for local industries, which are then induced to protect their interests by lobbying and corrupting public officials to maintain such restrictions. As Mauro points out, studies have shown that open economies usually boast lower corruption: "in other words, countries tend to be less corrupt when their trade is relatively free of government restrictions that corrupt officials can abuse."[50]
- **Subsidies:** Government-funded subsidies can become a source of rents when firms or companies for which they are not intended can appropriate them.
- **Price Controls:** Lowering the price of some good below its market value, usually for political reasons, creates incentives for individuals to bribe or otherwise influence government officials

to keep prices low or to acquire an unfair share of these goods at a below-market price.

- **Multiple Exchange Rates:** Some countries, Mauro notes, have many different exchange rates: one for importers, one for exporters, and another for investors, tourists, and so on. This encourages individuals to try to seek the most advantageous exchange rate, even where that rate would not normally apply. This type of policy is often associated with countries "with anti-competitive banking systems in which a key bank with government ties can make huge profits by arbitraging between markets," so that "if, for example, state-owned commercial banks ration scarce foreign exchange by allocating it according to priorities established by government officials, interested parties may be willing to bribe these officials to obtain more than their fair share."[51]

Corruption also has several negative consequences for government and international finance:

- **Prevents Economic Growth and Investment:** Perhaps the most damaging consequence of corruption is that it invariably lowers investment and inhibits economic growth. In corrupt environments, business people quickly learn that some sort of bribe is required for a project to get off the ground, and that corrupt bureaucrats are afterwards entitled a share in the profit. The cloak-and-dagger process of dealing with unscrupulous public officials, however, will generally decrease any incentive to invest in places where corruption is a normal way of doing business.
- **Misallocation of Talents:** Where corrupt behavior is encouraged, talented and educated individuals may be lured to engage in rent-seeking behavior rather than productive work, which will negatively affect the country's economic growth rate.
- **Loss of Tax Revenue:** In order to cover their tracks, corrupt officials will often engage in tax evasion and/or claim improper tax exemptions.

- **Budget Imbalances:** Lost or reduced tax revenue, along with increased public spending and improper lending practices by public or government-sponsored institutions at below-market interest rates (such as Fannie Mae and Freddie Mac) can lead to budget imbalances.
- **Lower Quality Public Infrastructure:** Handing out public contracts through a corrupt system might lead to bad or lower quality public infrastructure and/or services. The quality of public institutions can have a significant effect on GDP.
- **Distort Government Expenditure:** Widespread corruption may influence public officials to choose government expenditures less on the basis of their ability to increase the public good than for the opportunities they might provide for lucrative bribes or extortion. Extensive projects with complex budgets whose precise value may be difficult to ascertain, such as large infrastructure plans or high-tech defense systems, are often popular targets for corrupt practices.

The relationship between corruption and government is two-way: corruption undermines good government, while bad government encourages corruption. Corruption is therefore usually far worse in non-democratic countries and failed states than in democratic countries. The African Union, for instance, reports that the continent loses close to 25% of its GDP because of corruption,[52] And because of globalization corruption in these countries has a net effect on global finance as a whole.

What can be done? In an earlier chapter, we referred to Joseph Stiglitz's view that one of the benefits of globalization would be increased transparency: if governments want to succeed in a global economy, they will be forced to be more accountable and thus tougher on corruption. The need for increased accountability has led to the creation of non-governmental organizations like Transparency International, whose Corruption Perceptions Index (CPI) is now the standard for measuring the level of corruption in any given country. The Index measures corruption on a scale from 0–10, where 0 is the most corrupt and 10 the least. The 2011 study ranked 182 countries, and found that New Zealand is the least corrupt with a CPI score of 9.5, while North Korea tied with Somalia as the most corrupt (1); Canada ranks tenth (8.7) and the US twenty-fourth (7.1). Of the economically beleaguered PIIGS countries, Ireland is the least corrupt, ranking nineteenth overall with a CPI of 7.5, while Portugal is thirtieth (6.1) and Spain thirty-first (6.2).[53] Perhaps unsurprisingly, the two countries in the most economic trouble today are by far the most corrupt of the PIIGS nations: Italy ranks sixty-ninth with a CPI of 3.9, while Greece's 3.4 places it as low as eightieth.[54] Further analyses by Transparency International have shown that decreases in corruption means significant increases in both investment and GDP per capita. If the CPI of a country improves by one standard deviation (in this case, around 2.4) point, investment rates increase by more than 4%, while the annual growth rate of GDP per capita increases by over 0.5%. So any country that improves its CPI from, say 6 to 8, "will enjoy the benefits of an increase of 4 percentage points of investment, with consequent improvement in employment and economic growth."[55]

So the increased transparency that comes with globalization can also lead to a decrease in corruption. But there is another, more immediate and practical solution to avoiding the various problems associated with bureaucracy and corruption: governments must find ways to reduce the size of the public sector. While governments will always have a role to play in our lives, depending on the public sector alone to create economic development and prosperity creates more problems than solutions. As we have seen, large bureaucracies can lead to the monopolization of resources and other economic decisions that hinder innovation and fail to produce higher levels of income and investment. Governments need to find a maximal size that corresponds to a maximized potential for growth. According to a January 2012 paper by Spanish economists António Afonso and João Tovar Jalles, economic progress is "limited when government is zero percent of the economy (absence of rule of law, property rights, etc.), but also when it is closer to 100 percent (the law of diminishing returns operates in addition to, e.g., increased taxation required to finance the government's growing burden—which has adverse effects on human economic behavior, namely on consumption decisions)."[56] Finding a golden mean between these two extremes should be a top priority for governments today. But approaching this ideal between extremes will require some hard and unpopular decisions about rolling back the public sector. And the fact that politicians must be willing to commit political suicide for the social good is deeply sad and ironic, since the whole reason we elect representatives in the first place is precisely to protect the public good.

Smaller Is Better

Studies have also shown that governments not only should do more with less, but that many smaller governments actually outperform their big government counterparts economically. Between 2003 and 2012, countries with small governments reported a real GDP growth of 3.1% per year, as compared to 2.0% for big-government countries.[57]

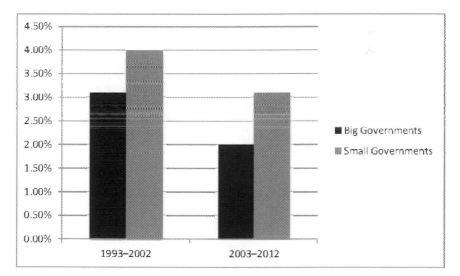

Figure 4–2: GDP growth in small vs. large governments, 1993–2012[58]

In addition, we might expect that big governments with a correspondingly large public sector have better social outcomes in heath care and education since they devote more of their resources and infrastructure to these outcomes. But this is not the case: the available data actually suggests that countries with small governments do no worse than big governments when it comes to social outcomes. Though big-government countries fared better than small-government countries with input metrics like student-pupil ratio in the education sector, small-government countries showed more success in output categories like academic achievement and student success: in mathematics, sciences, and overall literacy, students from small-government countries generally fare better than their big-government peers. The same goes for other social outcomes: over a nine-year period, employment growth was virtually identical between small- and big-government countries, as was youth unemployment; however, small-government countries fared slightly better with respect to the female demographic.[59] Although it isn't clear whether small government can be identified as the sole cause of better social outcomes, what is clear is that countries with smaller governments fare just as well as big-government countries when it comes to these outcomes.

Key Takeaways

- Governments today are finding it difficult to renegotiate their role in a globalized economy.

- Bad government policies are often informed by political factors, such as the desire to gain votes for election/re-election, rather than sound economic principles and practices.

- Government bailouts are NOT an effective solution to the current economic crisis.

- Austerity and stimulus packages are equally harmful and misguided. Neither approach has provided a viable solution to economic hardship.

- "The boom, not the slump, is the right time for austerity."

- Historically and statistically, raising taxes on the rich is not good economic policy. A higher tax on the rich produces disincentives, doesn't create higher revenue, and won't generate enough income to pull us out of a recession.

- Tax reform is necessary: governments must close loopholes in existing tax codes while avoiding the tendency to over-regulate.

- Government social policy must also be reformed in the face of an aging global population and the increased future cost of entitlement programs.

- Bureaucracy and corruption are two of the biggest threats to the global economy today.

- Large bureaucratic infrastructures often encourage "rent-seeking" behaviour.

- Smaller is better: research has shown that less bureaucracy and less corruption significantly increase economic growth.

ENDNOTES

[1] *Wikipedia*, "Financial Crisis of 2007–08," 7 November 2012.
<http://en.wikipedia.org/wiki/Financial_crisis_of_2007–2008>

[2] John B. Taylor, "The Financial Crisis and the Policy Responses: An Empirical Analysis of What Went Wrong," 2008.
<http://www.stanford.edu/~johntayl/FCPR.pdf>

[3] Warren Buffet, "To the Shareholders of Berkshire Hathaway Inc.," 2011.
<http://www.berkshirehathaway.com/letters/2011ltr.pdf>

[4] BBC News, "Follow the Money," 10 September 2009.
<http://news.bbc.co.uk/2/hi/business/8249411.stm>

[5] Walter Bagehot, *Lombard Street: A Description of the Money Market*, 1873.
<http://www.econlib.org/library/Bagehot/bagLom.html>

[6] Greenberg interviewed in *Frontline: Inside the Meltdown*, dir. by Michael Kirk, Season 27, Episode 4, 2009.

[7] Emergency Economic Stabilization Act (GovTrack), 3 October 2008.
<http://www.govtrack.us/congress/bills/110/hr1424/text>

[8] CBC News, "Banks Got $114B from Governments During Recession," 30 April 2012. <http://www.cbc.ca/news/business/story/2012/04/30/bank-bailout-ccpa.html>

[9] Ibid.

[10] Ibid.

[11] John McCain and Tom Coburn, "100 Wasteful Stimulus Projects That Actually Cost America Jobs," *Business Insider*, 2010. <http://www.businessinsider.com/mccain-100-wasteful-stimulus-projects-2010-8?op=1>

[12] Jay Makarenko, "Events Leading to the Liberal-NDP Coalition," *Mapleleafweb*, 18 December 2008. <http://www.mapleleafweb.com/features/events-leading-liberal-ndp-coalition-agreement>

[13] Office of the Auditor General of Canada, *The Fall 2011 Report of the Auditor General of Canada*, 2011. <http://www.oag-bvg.gc.ca/internet/English/parl_oag_201111_01_e_35933.html>

[14] Les Wittington and Bruce Campion-Smith, "Stimulus Package Worth $35B," *Toronto Star*, 27 January 2009. <http://www.thestar.com/news/canada/federalbudget/article/578084--stimulus-package-worth-35b>

[15] CBC News, "Impact of $47B Stimulus Minimal," 23 March 2010. <http://www.cbc.ca/news/canada/story/2010/03/23/fraser-institute-report.html>

[16] Bill Curry, "Ottawa's Long-Term Debt Plans Shelved," *Globe and Mail*, 25 October 2012. <http://www.theglobeandmail.com/news/politics/ottawas-long-term-debt-plans-shelved/article4649919/>

[17] Keynes qtd. in "Keynes was Right," by Paul Krugman, *New York Times*, 29 December 2011. <http://www.nytimes.com/2011/12/30/opinion/keynes-was-right.html>

[18] Mike Dorning, "Obama Channels Economic Frustration with $447 Billion Plan to Boost Jobs," *Bloomberg*, 9 September 2011. <http://www.bloomberg.com/news/2011-09-08/obama-proposes-cutting-payroll-taxes-in-half.html>

[19] Suzy Khimm, "The Sequester, Explained," *Washington Post*, 14 September 2012. <http://www.washingtonpost.com/blogs/ezra-klein/wp/2012/09/14/the-sequester-explained/>

[20] Les Wittington and Bruce Campion-Smith, "Federal Budget 2012: Tories Pinch Penny, Slash Spending in Fiscal Overhaul," *Toronto Star*, 30 March 2012. <http://www.thestar.com/news/canada/politics/article/1153617--federal-budget-2012-tories-pinch-penny-slash-spending-in-fiscal-overhaul>

[21] Warren Buffet, "Stop Coddling the Rich," *New York Times*, 14 August 2011. <http://www.nytimes.com/2011/08/15/opinion/stop-coddling-the-super-rich.html?adxnnl=1&adxnnlx=1347988129-XjuGq6mOFUZi9jV/Vw7OKQ>

[22] Barack Obama qtd. in "How Not to Grow a Wall Street Economy," *Wall Street Journal*, 21 August 2011. <http://online.wsj.com/article/SB10001424053111903327904576522382504681992.html>

[23] Danielle Kucera, Sanat Vallikappan, and Christine Harper, "Facebook Co-Founder Saverin Gives Up US Citizenship Before IPO," *Bloomberg*, 11 May 2012. <http://www.bloomberg.com/news/2012-05-11/facebook-co-founder-saverin-gives-up-u-s-citizenship-before-ipo.html>

[24] Daniel J. Mitchell, "The Historical Lessons of Lower Tax Rates," The Heritage Foundation, 13 August 2003. <http://www.heritage.org/research/reports/2003/08/the-historical-lessons-of-lower-tax-rates>

[25] Ibid.

[26] J. D. Foster, "Tax Policy: Obama Is Still Wrong on Tax Rates," The Heritage Foundation, 26 November 2012. <http://www.heritage.org/research/reports/2012/11/tax-policy-obama-is-still-wrong-on-tax-rates?rel=Taxes>

[27] Mitchell, 13 August 2003.

[28] Allistair Heath, "If You Want the Rich to Pay More Tax, Let Them Grow Even Richer," *The Telegraph*, 25 September 2012. <http://www.telegraph.co.uk/journalists/allister-heath/9565986/If-you-want-the-rich-to-pay-more-tax-let-them-grow-even-richer.html>

[29] Ibid.

[30] Foster, 26 November 2012.

[31] Robert Carroll and Gerald Plante, *Long-Run Macroeconomic Impact of Increasing Tax Rates on High-Income Taxpayers in 2013*, July 2012. <http://www.s-corp.org/wp-content/uploads/2012/07/EY-Study-Long-run-macroeconomic-impact-of-increasing-tax-rates-on-high-income-taxpayers-in-2013-2012-07-16-FINAL.pdf>

[32] David Koncieniewski, "US Has High Tax Rates but Pays Less," *New York Times*. 2 May 2011. <http://www.nytimes.com/2011/05/03/business/economy/03rates.html>

[33] Ibid.

[34] Yardeni qtd. in "The Growing Cost of an Aging World" by Brian Milner and Heather Scofield, *Globe and Mail*, 23 August 2012. <http://m.theglobeandmail.com/report-on-business/the-growing-cost-of-an-aging-world/article1211265/?service=mobile>

[35] Milner and Scofield, 23 August 2012.

[36] Ibid.

[37] Nicholas Eberstadt, "Are Entitlements Corrupting Us? Yes, American Character Is at Stake," *Wall Street Journal*, 31 August 2012. <http://online.wsj.com/article/SB10000872396390444914904577619671931313542.html>

[38] US Census Bureau, *Statistical Abstract of the United States*, 2012. <http://www.census.gov/compendia/statab/2012/tables/12s0539.pdf>

[39] Eberstadt, 31 August 2012.

[40] George F. Will, "Government: The Redistributionist Behemoth," *Washington Post*, 6 January 2012. <http://www.washingtonpost.com/opinions/government-the-redistributionist-behemoth/2012/01/05/gIQAFqqpfP_story.html>

[41] Congressional Budget Office, *Trends in the Distribution of Household Income Between 1979 and 2007*, 25 October 2011. <http://cbo.gov/publication/42729>

[42] Robert Pear, "Top Earners Doubled Nations Share of Income, Study Finds," *New York Times*, 25 October 2011. <http://www.nytimes.com/2011/10/26/us/politics/top-earners-doubled-share-of-nations-income-cbo-says.html?_r=0>

[43] The World Bank, *Golden Growth: Restoring the Lustre of the European Economic Model*, 2012. <http://siteresources.worldbank.org/ECAEXT/Resources/258598-1284061150155/7383639-1323888814015/8319788-1326139457715/fulltext_ch7.pdf>

[43] Matthew McClearn, "Retirement Age in Canada Rising," *Canadian Business*, 27 March 2012. <http://www.canadianbusiness.com/business-strategy/retirement-age-in-canada-rising/>

[44] The World Bank, 2012.

[45] Ibid.

[46] Ibid., "Empowering the Poor to Fight Corruption," 2011. <http://go.worldbank.org/APAR27YJ50>

[47] Paolo Mauro, "Why Worry about Corruption," International Monetary Fund, February 1997. <http://www.imf.org/external/pubs/ft/issues6/index.htm>

[48] NHLnumbers.com, "Pittsburgh Penguins (12/13)," N.d. <http://stats.nhlnumbers.com/teams/PIT?year=2013>

[49] Mauro, February 1997.

[50] Ibid.

[51] Ibid.

[52] Hadhek Zouhaier, "Corruption, Investment and Economic Growth," *International Journal of Economic Research*, Vol. 2, No. 5, 2011.

[53] Transparency International, *Corruption Perceptions Index 2011*, November 2011. <http://cpi.transparency.org/cpi2011/results/>.

[54] Ibid.

[55] Ibid.

[56] António Afonso and João Tovar Jalles, "Economic Performance, Government Size, and Institutional Quality," January 2012. <https://editorialexpress.com/cgi-bin/conference/download.cgi?db_name=IIPF68&paper_id=355>

[57] Ryan Bourne and Thomas Oechsle, "Small Is Best: Lessons from Advanced Economies," UK Centre for Policy Studies, May 2012. <http://www.cps.org.uk/files/reports/original/120522105633-smallisbest.pdf>

[58] Ibid.

[59] Ibid.

Chapter Five

THE MISBEHAVIOR OF BANKS

"The study of money, above all other fields in economics, is one in which complexity is used to disguise truth or to evade truth, not to reveal it." – John Kenneth Galbraith

IN OUR PREVIOUS chapters, we've seen numerous examples of how banks have contributed to our current economic crisis. In the case of the US housing bubble, banks used their power and influence to take advantage of government policy, creating a toxic situation that helped spur a broader crisis from which we are still trying to recover. In what follows, we will focus on two broad themes—regulation and credit cards—and various sub-themes related to them, such as the controversies surrounding the Glass-Steagall Act, increased deregulation, derivatives, the rise of exchange-traded funds, and how credit cards have become a means for banks to reap huge financial rewards while putting individuals further into debt.

No matter how customer-oriented banks present themselves as, I believe that they care very little about the people whom they serve. Banks typically abuse the trust placed in them by the general public and by governments, often by disguising their misdeeds in complicated instruments and methods of analysis. An appalling lack of transparency allows banks to take advantage of the public's lack of knowledge; working behind the curtain, such institutions eat away at your savings through prohibitively high service fees. This chapter hopes to be a little like Dorothy's Toto, pulling back the curtain to reveal how large banks played their part in hastening the current recession. I hope that you will leave this chapter with a better understanding of just how these institutions operate, and adopt a more cautious attitude in your day-to-day dealings with the banks.

A Brief History of (De)Regulation

The economic crisis of recent years has raised serious questions about the adequacy of existing regulatory frameworks, both in the US and all over the world. The crisis has revealed a number of shocking weaknesses within these regulatory structures, including poor risk assessment, irresponsible lending practices, and a lack of transparency and accountability that has endangered both the banks themselves and the public at large. This section offers a brief history of bank regulation prior to the crisis, focusing specifically on the US. Grasping the historical relationship between banks and government regulation will help you to come to grips with the how's and whys of current problems.

In the lead-up to the housing crisis, the US government implemented policies that opened the door for banks to take on predatory loaning practices. After implementing these policies, the government trusted the banks to do the right things to make the "ownership society" happen. The US government assumed that the big banks and financial institutions would police themselves. It was assumed that, in the absence of firm regulations, the need for self-survival would curtail financial institutions from excessive risk-taking. The idea of the free-market system as self-regulating and self-correcting is an integral part of the economic theory of globalization; yet too much confidence in this view sometimes blinds governments and banks to the fact that their actions have real consequences beyond abstract mathematical models and the shuffling of papers between offices. We are now paying the price for placing too much trust in institutions whose goals are driven less by social responsibility and good business sense than by excessive greed.

1913-1979: The Push for Regulation and the Glass-Steagall Act

Prior to the twentieth century, the US economic system was barely regulated and was therefore vulnerable to frequent market panics. Between the Civil War and World War I, the economy suffered through no less than three major panics, in 1873, 1893, and 1907. To curtail further collapses, both state and federal legislators set about implementing a number of financial reforms. After the 1907 panic, which saw the failure of several large trust companies and massive account withdrawals by spooked bank customers, a Congress-led commission proposed the creation of the Federal Reserve. The Federal Reserve Act (1913) established a system of nationally chartered banks for each region of the country. All nationally chartered banks were required to "join the system and permitted state chartered banks to do so, if they fulfilled all federal regulations—such as levels of required reserves and restrictions on risky investments—which tended to be stricter than those imposed by state statutes."[1] Around the same time, a number of private regulating entities began to emerge at the state level, such as clearing houses and state banking associations, that would impose "codes of conduct on the behavior of members."[2]

But the creation of the Federal Reserve alone wasn't enough to prevent market crashes throughout the 1920s and 1930s. After the failures of thousands of banks during the Great Depression (1929–1933), the Federal Reserve was forced to change the structure of financial regulation. In January 1932, Congress passed the Reconstruction Finance Corporation Act (RFC), which would extend loans to all chartered banks in the US, including those that had no direct links to the Federal Reserve. A month later, Congress further expanded the Federal Reserve's loaning powers by passing the Banking Act, which was co-authored by Senator Carter Glass and then-chairman of the House Committee on Banking and Currency, Henry Steagall. The Banking Act allowed the Feds to loan money not only to member banks but also to individuals, firms, and corporations under the stipulation that borrowers prove they could not acquire loans from the commercial banks in their own communities.

The Banking Act led to the creation of the Glass-Steagall Act, which was passed into law in the summer of 1933. Both Glass and Steagall had already introduced banking reforms in the years previous. In 1931, Glass introduced legislation that called for a unified national banking system, the restriction of commercial bankers to the banking business, increased liability for any misconduct by commercial bankers, and the enforcement of increased government regulation. For his part, Steagall sought to protect investors by introducing national deposit insurance. Their respective bills both passed through the House of Representatives between 1931 and 1932, and were eventually combined into a single bill that included most of Glass' regulations and Steagall's deposit insurance.

The Glass-Steagall Act would significantly shape the US economic system for decades to come. The importance of the act can be divided into three major provisions:

1. **Nationalized Deposit-Insurance:** The act led to nationalized deposit insurance and the creation of the Federal Deposit Insurance Corporation (FDIC). All banks insured by the FDIC were now legally obligated to submit a quarterly report of condition and income. The FDIC would then be responsible for maintaining this data, checking its accuracy, and making it public.

2. **Separation of Commercial from Investment Banking:** As Alejandro Komai and Gary Richardson comment, the Glass-Steagall Act "required commercial banks to sell their securities affiliates within one year and restricted their bond departments to the purchase and sale of securities on the order of and for the account of customers. Underwriting investment securities was prohibited."[3] In short, Glass-Steagall guaranteed a buffer zone between the practices of Main Street commercial banks and Wall Street investment firms.

3. **Increased Regulation:** The act placed important limits and regulations on the behavior of financial institutions. These regulations imposed increased transparency on member banks by requiring officers and directors to report all borrowing from other organizations, and a mandatory increase in minimum capital requirements, or the minimum amount of capital that a bank needs to hold to operate when it suffers losses. Further changes included restricting the use of bank credit for speculation, increased authority for bank examiners, and the federal supervision of group banking.[4]

Another important policy emerged from the subsequent passage of the Securities Act in 1933. The Securities Act established the Securities and Exchange Commission (SEC), which would regulate the issuing, purchase, and sale of securities, credit certificates, the ownership of stocks or bonds, or the right to ownership connected with tradable derivatives. Not unlike the creation of the FDIC, the SEC legally required all public companies to submit regular financial statements. Most importantly, the new regulations catalyzed by the Glass-Steagall Act restricted banks' risk-taking activities.

1980–1995: Repeal of Glass-Steagall and the Savings and Loan Crisis

The regulatory structures instituted after the Great Depression helped stabilize the marketplace for the better part of fifty years. With the push towards globalization in the 1980s and 1990s, however, the structure of financial regulation changed significantly. According to Komai and Richardson, the impetus for this change came from the following directions:

- The emergence and prevalence of free-market thinking in policy debates.
- The pressure on US financial institutions to compete in an international marketplace against institutions "operating in more permissive regulatory environments." Hence, "US institutions

incessantly lobbied to loosen regulations and level the playing field."[5]

▪ The collapse of savings and loans (S&L) institutions during the 1970s. S&Ls used federally insured, low-interest deposits to fund mortgages. Their collapse occurred in part because policies, created during the Great Depression, regulated the S&L industry to function "in an environment with low and stable inflation"; hence, regulators had capped interest rates (known as "Regulation Q") on both home loans and savings deposits at 6%. But when inflation rose well above 6% during the late 1970s, many S&Ls became insolvent.[6]

I've already discussed some of the effects of the first two factors in previous chapters. Here, I want to focus specifically on the S&L crisis, which clearly demonstrates the give-an-inch, take-a-mile mentality of many banking institutions.

When the S&Ls went bankrupt, industry lobbyists went to work on politicians, pressuring Congress to remove the restrictions that had forced them into bankruptcy. The problem, according to the banks, was the Glass-Steagall Act. Glass-Steagall restricted commercial banks' participation in the money markets and limited their ability to compete with investment banks. For years, deregulation gradually opened a space for a secondary, "shadow" banking system to emerge alongside the more traditional commercial banks. This system was prominently made up of the major investment banks, whose market activities mostly operated beyond the reach of regulators. Feeling left behind, commercial banks moved to ease regulations so as to better compete with their "shadowy" counterparts.

Pressure from the commercial banking industry eventually led to what monetary policy consultant Bert Ely calls "an incomplete and bungled deregulation of S&Ls."[7] This bungled deregulation spurred one of the biggest financial scandals in US history. In 1980 and 1982, the government lifted regulations on the kinds of investments that S&Ls were typically allowed to make. After the passage of the Depository Institutions Deregulation and Monetary Control and Garn-St. Germain

Depository Institutions Acts (1980, 1982), S&Ls were now granted the power to offer a wider variety of financial services. At the time, then-Federal Reserve chairman Alan Greenspan and other regulators believed that financial institutions had strong incentives to protect their shareholders. The institutions would therefore "regulate themselves through improved risk management" through the use of "analysts, credit rating agencies, and investors."[8] In a 1997 speech before Congress, Greenspan stated that these steps towards financial "modernization" were necessary to "remove outdated restrictions that serve no useful purpose, that decrease economic efficiency, and that . . . limit choices and options for the consumer of financial services." Removing regulations "would permit banking organizations to compete more effectively in their natural markets. The result would be a more efficient financial system providing better services to the public."[9]

However, increased deregulation also expanded the S&Ls lending authority in ways that made lending practices both difficult to supervise and excessively risky. They began investing in increasingly risky ventures, such as commercial real estate lending and junk bonds. Relaxed accounting rules also gave the S&Ls more leeway when reporting their actual financial situation, creating an environment ripe for corruption and fraud. Further deregulatory acts led to budget cuts to the Federal Home Loan Bank Board (FHLBB). With their newfound freedom from regulation and weakened supervision by the FHLBB, the S&Ls crafted a number of accounting gimmicks that not only "violated generally accepted accounting principles," but also allowed them to "operate with less and less real capital."[10] Emboldened by deregulation, the S&Ls "took on more risk, they had a smaller capital cushion to fall back on and, therefore, less to lose by making bad decisions."[11] In turn, most of the S&L industry treated deregulation as an excuse to turn the market into their personal playground. Typically, it was the taxpayers who paid the price for bankers' reckless behavior. As Bert Ely points out, "by the end of 2004, the direct cost of the S&L crisis to taxpayers was $124 billion."[12]

One of the better known examples of the corruption that fostered the S&L crisis was the failure of Lincoln Savings and Loan and the criminal charges levied against its chairman, Charles Keating Jr. Prior to Keating, Lincoln Savings and Loan was a modestly run company, with nearly half of its assets invested in home loans and only a quarter of assets considered at risk. After taking over the company and firing management, Keating remodeled Lincoln Savings and Loan's business practices to reflect the increasing deregulation of the S&L associations in 1980 and 1982. From 1984 to 1988, Keating directly invested federally insured S&L deposits in risky land purchases, commercial real estate ventures, and junk bonds. Lincoln Savings' assets jumped from $1.1 billion to $5.5 billion in just four years. This remarkable growth led to an investigation by the FHLBB. Keating responded by pumping up campaign contributions to five US senators, who subsequently intervened on his behalf. As a result, the FHLBB backed down from pursuing legal action.

However, the federal government eventually seized Lincoln Savings, and regulators charged Keating with a $1.1-billion fraud and racketeering lawsuit in 1989. Earlier that same year, the American Continental Corporation, the Keating-run parent company of Lincoln Savings, went bankrupt. More than twenty-one thousand investors lost their life savings, and the seizure of Lincoln Savings alone would end up costing taxpayers upwards of $2 billion. Keating was eventually sent to prison for five years.

A sales document written by Keating to his employees prior to the scandal sums up his attitude towards the general investor: "always remember the weak, meek and ignorant are always good targets."[13] Unfortunately, this kind of attitude is not limited to brazen charlatans like Keating. The trouble is, targeting consumers who do not understand the convoluted machinations of the banking industry has pretty much become the standard approach for commercial and investment banks alike. The S&L crisis demonstrated a simple, unfortunate, fact about what happens when many financial institutions are given too much freedom: if you give them an inch, they won't just take a mile, they'll take twenty.

1996-2012: Deregulation *Redux*

By the mid-1990s, many of the larger commercial banks were operating more and more like investment banks. Banks needed to become both larger and more complex, it was argued, to deal with the expanding global economy. And as the financial sector grew, banks continued to put pressure on Congress to dismantle what was left of federal regulatory structures. In January 2011, the Financial Crisis Inquiry Commission reported that "from 1997 to 2008, the financial sector expended $2.7 billion in reported federal lobbying expenses; individuals and political action committees in the sector made more than $1 billion in campaign contributions" to fight for deregulation.[14] Greenspan and then-treasury secretary Robert Rubin continued to push the belief that the market would self-regulate and that the inherent self-interest of market participants would generate regulation without the need for any kind of government intervention.

Finally, in 1999, Glass-Steagall was repealed. The death of Glass Steagall was a symbolic victory for the radical deregulation movement, which had lobbied for years to eliminate the gap between Main Street and Wall Street. The result, however, was not some utopia in which banks magically regulated themselves and innovated out of fear of losing their hard-won reputation, but "a 21st-century financial system" operating with "19th-century safeguards." The repeal opened the door for bank megamergers, and the period between 1990 and 2005 saw approximately seventy-four such mergers between banks with assets of over $10 billion each, while the ten largest went from owning 25% of industry assets to 55%.[15] The repeal also opened the door for Congress to pass the Commodities Futures Modernization Act of 2000, which further reduced already-weakened oversight, reporting, and reserve regulations. The Commodities Futures Act deregulated over-the-counter or off-market derivatives—that is, the act made it possible to trade stocks, bonds, commodities, or derivatives directly between two parties, rather than through the stock exchange. In turn, the Commodities Futures Act effectively banned regulators from even *looking* into the risks entailed by over-the-counter derivatives, essentially giving the banks free reign to do what they will. I discuss derivatives in more detail below; for the time being, what is important to understand is that the repeal of Glass-Steagall made it possible for things like the Commodities Futures Act to exist, opening the door for even further problems down the road.

Over the last thirty-odd years, the financial sector has managed to gradually remove most of the safeguards established at the beginning of the twentieth century. To be sure, some of these regulations needed updating in light of broader changes in national and global economic systems. Regulation Q, for example, was clearly inadequate to deal with the dramatic changes in interest rates and increased inflation of the 1960s. But updating existing regulations is not the same as dissolving or simply ignoring them, which in many cases is precisely what seems to have occurred.

In July of 2012, Sanford Weill, the former chairman of Citigroup, stated that the US should separate investment banking from commercial banking, essentially arguing for the reimplementation of the Glass-Steagall, which was in fact repealed with Mr. Weill's help. The hypocrisy is almost too much to bear. Citigroup's dealings, like many of the giants of Wall Street, were full of conflicts of interest because Citigroup had fought to integrate investment banking and commercial banking. It was not uncommon for Citigroup to lend to companies and then promote those same companies to its investors. You'd think that after a devastating financial crisis, banks would ease up on their self-serving lobbying, but that has not been the case.

As an example, the Dodd-Frank Wall Street Reform and Consumer Protection Act (2010) has not helped to secure large deposits and has not succeeded in limiting banks' risky transactions. Even with quite a lot of freedom still in the hands of the financial sector, US banks have campaigned to undercut the Dodd-Frank reforms, which would restrict unnecessary risks taken by bankers. Banks have also campaigned against new international rules developed by the Basel Committee on Banking

Supervision that would require banks to increase the amount of capital they keep in reserve over a period of time as a means to prepare for potential crises.[16]

Quite simply, the banks' efforts to avoid regulation verge on the absurd. Take, for instance, the Institute for International Finance, a banking lobby group. In September of 2011, the Institute issued a press release claiming, "there is an acute danger that the pursuit of financial stability imposes too great a cost on economic growth and job creation at a fragile time for the world economy."[17] I'm willing to bet that everyone, including the super-rich, support the pursuit of "financial stability." The sad thing is that the new regulations aren't even excessive. The regulations ask banks to increase their core capital to 7% of their assets from the current 2%. Large banks, because their collapse would be more devastating and pose a greater threat, would have to reserve capital up to 9.5%. Banks would also have to have enough cash and easily sold assets on hand to survive thirty days of a market crisis, and their core capital would have to equal at least 3% of their total assets.[18] These new rules install much-needed safeguards designed to pull in the reins after the banks had let the system get so out of control. But banks want to be able to continue using every available cent to increase profit rather than ensure stability.

But rather than listen to the banks, we should push for even further reform. Banks should not be permitted to engage in activities, like derivatives trading, which cannot be easily examined by regulators. Financial products and services continue to evolve and become ever more complicated largely to benefit the elite and confuse everyone else.

Excessive Profit at the Expense of Customers

The sense that financial services are no longer customer oriented is a lament heard recently in a letter of resignation written by a Goldman Sachs employee and made public in the *New York Times*. In March 2012, Greg Smith resigned as a Goldman Sachs executive director and head of the firm's US equity derivatives business in Europe, the Middle East, and Africa after nearly twelve years at the firm. In his letter, Mr. Smith faulted a change in corporate attitude as the primary reason for his resignation. He stated that the culture had changed from one in which the client and his or her needs were valued, to one in which making a profit at the expense of clients was paramount to all other concerns: "will people push the envelope and pitch lucrative and complicated products to clients even if they are not the simplest investments or the ones most directly aligned with the client's goals? Absolutely. Every day, in fact."[19] Mr. Smith also stated that he was ashamed of the behavior of his co-workers and did not approve of promotions based purely on how much a person made for the company. What Mr. Smith's letter indicates is that the incentives offered by banks to their employees only encourage greed and discourage honesty. And when employees are motivated by personal greed, it becomes much more likely that clients will suffer.

This was also the case at J. P. Morgan, Chase & Co. Of the ten largest US fund companies, J. P. Morgan was the only one that focused on selling mutual funds it had created. Brokers were pressured to sell J. P. Morgan's proprietary products to their customers, regardless of whether or not they were a good fit for their clients' needs or if other options would perform better or cost less. This practice benefited J. P. Morgan at the expense of its investors, since the bank could collect fees (and actually charged higher than average fees) for managing assets in their funds.

How did they get away with this? As it stands, the US securities laws make way for brokers to give their clients investment advice that is not in their best interest because the laws do not impose a fiduciary duty on them. Brokers need only suggest "suitable" investments. This clears the way for employees to be swayed by bonuses, commissions, and other rewards. But compensation becomes even more preposterous as you climb the ladder and set your eyes on the earnings of Wall Street CEOs. Given their contributions, CEOs' huge pay increases and bonuses are undeserved. Generally bank CEOs are not exceptional leaders or managers. Rather, they merely maintain the status quo of guaranteed profit-making machines.

In truth, any nominally managed bank is guaranteed to be profitable because the financial services distribution system overwhelmingly works in favor of banks and against the interests of consumers, most of whom are financially illiterate. As consumers, we are placed on an uneven playing field with banks in the money game. Even if banks abuse us, we cannot win because we could never afford to take a bank to court. Ultimately, financial stability has little to do with the banks or their CEOs; rather, stability is determined by the regulatory structures in place. Canada was able to avoid failures experienced in the US thanks to stringent regulations imposed on its banks, not because their CEOs were better managers than their US counterparts.

As we have already seen, many bank CEOs have benefited from dishonest financial practices. The creation of financial instruments out of nowhere, creating phantom wealth, contributed to the worldwide meltdown in 2008 and led to the most devastating recession since the Great Depression. To add insult to injury, taxpayers' money has often gone toward compensating CEOs and giving bonuses to employees for cheating their clients, behavior that is especially hard to swallow given that the notoriously too-big-to-fail US banks turned around and required money from bailouts.

The increasingly risk-addicted structure of today's banks also leaves investors vulnerable. Many people believe that banks make loans from the funds put into their hands for safekeeping. This makes logical sense. If Bob gives me money and I know he isn't going to ask for it for awhile, I can make some money by lending Bob's money to James and charging him interest. But make no mistake, banks do not run a logical business since they can make loans based simply on a debtor's promise to pay it off. So long as loans are repaid, no one loses. However, the movement towards deregulation has made it possible for banks to make loans when they do not actually have the money to back those loans. Banks can do this because depositors only occasionally withdraw physical currency, they rarely empty their accounts, and they almost never demand their money at the same time that every other depositor demands theirs. Though risky, most bank branches are willing to gamble on giving loans on the promise of repayment since the central banks will infuse local banks with funds if a banking panic should actually occur.

But the central banks cannot always cover these losses. We have seen the disastrous impact when depositors lose confidence and demand their money not only from local banks, but also from major investment firms. One of the most infamous examples of this occurred with the collapse of Lehman Brothers in 2008, the largest bankruptcy in American history. Before declaring bankruptcy, Lehman was the fourth largest investment bank in America. But rumors about Lehman left investors worried about their funds. And when worry turned to panic, investors liquidated their accounts, causing the bank to collapse.

So why did this happen? What might have started the rumors that led to such a loss in confidence? Lehman borrowed significant resources to fund its investing practices in the years leading to its bankruptcy in 2008, a process called leveraging. Large portions of Lehman's investments were in housing-related assets, so it was vulnerable to a downturn in the housing market. One measure of this risk-taking was its leverage ratio, the ratio of assets to owner's equity. Between 2003 and 2007, the leverage ratio increased from 24:1 to 31:1. Although this ratio made it possible for Lehman to generate incredible profits during the housing boom, it also meant that a small decline of 3% to 4% in the value of its assets would virtually eliminate its book value or equity. Lehman Brothers was able to get away with taking such a risk because investment banks were no longer subject to the same kinds of regulations as commercial depository banks.

It's not as though banks operate in complete chaos—there are rules to the risky game banks play when lending unavailable funds—but today these rules allow for far too much leeway. Banks have to abide by the rules of the fractional-reserve system, the dominant system used worldwide, which means they can maintain cash reserves that are a fraction of their customers' deposits. When funds are deposited into a bank, a bank need only keep a fraction (the reserve ratio) of the amount as reserves and can loan out the rest. When funds lent out are deposited in another bank, this action increases the deposits of the second bank, which makes room for further lending. Since most bank deposits are treated as money, fractional-reserve banking increases money supplies so that banks are essentially creating money. The fractional-reserve system allows banks to loan $9 for every $1 it holds in reserve. That might not seem like much, but consider that hundreds of thousands of dollars that don't exist can be created this way. Accordingly, the money supply of a country ends up being larger than the amount of money created by the country's central bank.

Derivatives

A wealthy investment banker arrives home one evening and notices his young daughter drawing crude pictures of US currency on various pieces of scrap paper. After a few minutes, the daughter notices her father watching her and hands him a handful of crayon-green play money. The father smiles and takes out a large billfold of real money from his pocket and hands her a few dollars.

"Dad, how do you make so much money?," the daughter asks.

"That's easy, Mary," he replies, "I just create financial papers, like derivatives!"

"But, Dad!," says Mary worriedly, "Don't the police catch people who make fake money?"

"Don't worry, dear. What I do is legal. You see, nobody understands my financial papers. Not politicians, not prosecutors, not police, not even investors."

"Then I can use my crayons to color papers to make money too!"

"No, no Mary. You see, people understand your drawings. They know your 'money' has no real value. But because nobody understands my papers, I can call it 'valuable' and people have no choice but to believe me!"

This little anecdote well describes a prevailing attitude among banks when it comes to derivatives: since no one but the bankers understands them, they can dictate whether or not they're valuable, and we're pretty much forced to believe them. You might have heard that derivatives had a significant part to play in the financial crisis; indeed, the meltdown of the US real estate market was arguably caused by the multi-layered securitization of mortgages in the form of derivatives. The foreclosure of homes wrapped up in mortgage derivatives became a huge problem: it was impossible to know which mortgages fell under which derivatives. The complexity and secrecy around modern derivatives has emerged from commercial banks' desire to compete with investment banks. Since competitors immediately copy new products, traders must be constantly innovating to maintain revenue by increasing volumes or creating new structures. Complexity delays competition, prevents clients from unbundling products, and generally reduces transparency. As briefly mentioned above, most derivatives also avoid regulations by being sold over-the-counter through private trades instead of through public stock or commodity exchanges. So investment banks can make deals without having to comply with trade rules sanctioned by exchange supervisors.

We know that derivatives are a sneaky business, but how are they related to the financial crisis? In the early 1990s, J. P. Morgan created a kind of derivative called credit default swaps (CDS) in an effort to hedge their loan risks. These CDSs essentially offered insurance, creating a contract between a buyer and a seller to cover a specific bond or loan. The buyer pays for coverage and then pays yearly premiums to cover losses on the face amount of the bond or loan.

A trade based on future values is not fundamentally determined by the performance of the market: everything is a gamble. CDSs allowed investors to make side bets; for example, with so much trade tied up in American dollars, foreign holders of US dollars need to feel pretty certain that the US Treasury bills they were buying wouldn't lose their value due to inflation or a falling dollar. So foreign holders would turn to the derivatives market, where they could buy a contract that would insure them against the rise in inflation. Alternatively, investors could buy contracts to insure themselves against the failure of large companies or price changes in commodities such as oil. Having this "quasi" insurance built investor confidence: investors continued to invest because they could make up for losses through derivatives.

Derivatives wouldn't pose any particular problems if they were used as a hedging device for those who actually held outstanding loans and bonds; derivatives could guarantee that the debts were repaid, but this was a strange kind of insurance. Since a CDS isn't exactly insurance, it isn't liable to the regulations of traditional insurance products. What makes a CDS different from an insurance contract is that an investor could buy a CDS on a specific company's bonds without actually owning that company's bonds. So investors could gamble on any number of situations in which their assets were not actually in harm's way; it would be like buying fire insurance on your neighbor's house.

With so little regulation, and so much to gain, risk speculators got in on the game. Those who wanted exposure to, say, subprime mortgage-backed securities, but who didn't actually own the underlying credits, were able to speculate on them. Speculators bought and sold trillions of dollars of insurance, betting that subprime mortgage pools would, or wouldn't, default. The bet could go either way. For example, those who thought a certain corporation wouldn't be able to repay its bondholders could speculate by buying CDSs on their bonds and would stand to gain if the corporation defaulted. Meanwhile, those who believed that that same corporation was in good shape could offer insurance to those who disagreed. If the corporation didn't default, those who collected premiums from investors who expected a default would come out ahead because they'd keep the premiums and not have to pay the insurance.

But when the financial crisis hit, investors, companies, and countries that had purchased derivatives found out that the insurance provided by the derivatives depended entirely on the strength of the "insurer." If the financial company that sold insurance against something couldn't pay, the derivative was worthless. The premium payments, as well as the insurance against default, would all disappear. Investors quickly realized that the derivatives market could not be depended on to fulfill its insurance promises.

The bankruptcy of Lehman Brothers and the near bankruptcy of American International Group (AIG) were so dangerous because they backed so much money through derivatives. Similarly, the Federal Reserve could not let Bear Stearns enter into bankruptcy because it had insured trillions of dollars in CDSs. If Bear Stearns collapsed, none of the banks or institutions insured by Bear Stearns' derivatives would be insured or hedged anymore. The firm would have to claim losses of billions of dollars that had been weighted at higher values because the money was insured against losses. Such a bank had become "too big to fail" since letting it fail would be utterly devastating; hence, taxpayers have had to carry the burden. Yet we see no change. Three years after AIG needed a taxpayer bailout of $182 billion because of insurance it issued on mortgage-backed securities, the market for CDSs still hasn't been made transparent.

(Un)Just Desserts

Most of the Wall Street titans who caused the crisis are unlikely to receive any kind of substantial legal punishment. They will likely make non-criminal plea settlements and get away with small fines relative to the profits they saw, and the losses endured by their clients. And, of course, there will be no real compensation for investors. So even though the conduct on Wall Street harmed more individuals than any common criminal, the executives who allowed and encouraged risky dealings will likely never see jail time. Outside of Charles Keating, not even one top executive from any of the firms that nearly brought down the financial system has spent a day in jail. Sure, some individuals have been charged for hiding billions in losses and/or lining their own pockets, but none have been punished for actions that benefited the corporations. What's worse, the prosecution efforts that are moving forward in response to the 2008 crisis are targeting homeowners for endorsing "fraudulent" loan applications, rather than the financial institutions that pushed the loans.

Can we hope that those responsible will at least pay for their crimes financially? Some of the largest US banks are facing massive lawsuits over mortgage securities worth tens of billions of dollars. In September 2011, the US Federal Housing Finance Agency (FHFA) launched a lawsuit against seventeen financial institutions, including Bank of America, Goldman Sachs, Deutsche Bank AG, J. P. Morgan, HSBC Holdings PLC, Barclays Bank PLC, and Nomura Securities Co. Ltd. The suit alleged that these banks had sold mortgage-backed securities improperly by misrepresenting the quality and risks of the investments. Apparently, mortgage-backed securities were sold to Fannie Mae and Freddie Mac without any indication of the level of risk the assets carried. As we already know, Fannie Mae and Freddie Mac lost over $30 billion from mortgage-backed securities and other assets during the credit crisis. The suit alleges that banks had pooled thousands of mortgages and sold them as securities without due diligence. The suit also claims that banks missed or ignored signs that many borrowers' incomes had been incorrectly reported to receive more or larger loans. It is also alleged that the banks inflated the percent of properties that were owner-occupied, that they understated the loan-to-value ratio, and that they ignored evidence that defective or questionable loans had been used in the securities.

The FHFA lawsuit will take years before it is resolved, and even then the banks' fines will be minimal compared to how much they gained and how much middle-class families lost. It's also possible that nothing will even be proven, and the banks will get off scot-free. So far, banks have been unwilling to accept any blame for their actions. In October 2011, Citigroup made a deal to pay $285 million to settle charges by the SEC that it misled investors. But the settlement with Citigroup notes that the bank agreed to resolve the matter "without admitting or denying" any wrongdoing. The SEC had claimed that Citigroup, along with other Wall Street giants like Goldman Sachs, sold investors $1-billion worth of derivatives that were linked to the US housing market in 2007 and then also bet against those investments.[20]

No-contest settlements may make it possible for cases to be resolved more quickly, but in most cases these settlements seem to be no more than a slap on the wrist. Defendants don't have to admit to anything that could cost them in future lawsuits from investors. And while Citigroup came to a resolution without accepting fault, in August 2012, Goldman Sachs was cleared of charges that they misled investors by suggesting that mortgage securities were a safe investment. Although the big banks are still under investigation and Goldman Sachs is still not completely free and clear, the decision comes as a disappointment and a setback for those middle-class Americans victimized by the financial sector.

Exchange-Traded Funds

Like the banking system in general, the rapid growth, increasing complexity, and constant pressure to innovate new types of investment products threaten the stability of the economic system. These factors are so widespread that even those investment products specifically designed to avoid excessive risk are becoming contaminated. One example of this is the rise of exchange-traded funds (ETFs). In theory, ETFs seem like a good idea: invented in the late 1980s at the Toronto Stock Exchange, ETFs combine aspects of traditional mutual funds (a bundle of diversified assets) with traditional stocks. Unlike mutual funds, which can only be traded at the end of the day, ETFs can be traded throughout the entire day like regular stocks. In this respect, ETFs boast several advantages over other kinds of investment products, such as lower marketing, distribution, and accounting costs; greater buying and selling flexibility; tax efficiency; and increased market exposure and diversification. In essence, ETFs are "cheap mutual fund[s]" that allow "retail investors access to diversified portfolios of assets that had previously been the sole preserve of institutional investors."[21] To put it simply: if you "shop wisely, you can . . . spread your money across low-fee ETFs that will give you access to just about all the worthwhile investments on earth, with no trading commission."[22]

Inexpensive, simple, and bearing the potential for greater returns than more traditional mutual funds like Registered Retirement Savings

Plans (RRSPs), ETFs have subsequently grown in popularity over the last several years. And in the wake of the 2008 financial crisis, ETFs have become more and more viable as an option for investors demanding lower risk portfolios. According to reports by Lyxor, Europe's largest provider of ETFs, ETF turnover on the European exchange accounted for 14% of market activity, up 6% from the year previous and four times the levels of 2008.[23] In the US, the number of on-market ETFs has exploded from 343 in 2006 to almost 1,100 in 2011, while global assets listed under ETFs are predicted to grow to nearly $4.7 trillion by 2015.

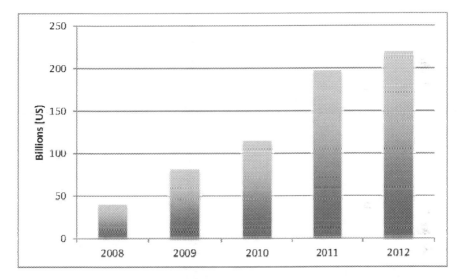

Figure 5–1: Total ETF assets in managed accounts, 2008–2012[24]

At the same time, however, ETF products have expanded well beyond simple "bundles" of tradable securities. As Brooke Masters points out in a 2011 article for the *Financial Times*, "today ETFs . . . do everything from tracking the price of gold or copper, to providing the inverse of the return on the Standard & Poor's 500, the world's most widely-tracked [stock] index."[25] Like other kinds of investment products pushed by banks, ETFs have developed a subset of products called "synthetics" that depend largely on "swaps and futures to provide promised returns rather than holding actual gold, shares or bonds."

Experimentation with and manipulation of the scope of ETFs by banks and other investment strategists has made this once low-risk portfolio option progressively riskier, drawing the attention of regulatory agencies like the US SEC and the European Systemic Risk Board.[26]

Along with increased risk, ETFs are not quite as cost-efficient as they might first appear. Annually, the management expenses associated with ETFs are relatively small, around 0.25% to 0.5%. However, ETF strategists also take their cut, usually anywhere from 0.1% to 1.25%. Add another 0.1% to 1.25% for custodial fees, 0.15% for transaction costs, and anywhere from 0.3% to 1% in fees from unscrupulous investment advisors, and an ETF can end up costing you upwards of 3% of your assets annually. Although these costs are similar to those attached to regular mutual fund portfolios, most of the costs of the latter come from the expense of managing the underlying assets, whereas the underlying assets of an ETF usually cost less than 1%. In short, bankers are exploiting the popularity of ETFs to introduce a number of different "layers" of fees to get between you and your money.[27]

Another concern posed by the rise of ETFs is the practice of what investment strategists call "backtesting." Since the buying and selling of ETFs didn't really take off until 2008–2009, they have a very short performance history, which makes it difficult to assess their long-term value. According to Canadian investment research firm Morningstar, fully one third of the 485 ETF strategists tracked by the firm have less than three years of performance history.[28] But if investment bankers are anything, they're shrewd. Realizing that a lack of historically demonstrable performance might cause some investors to avoid ETF-managed portfolios, bankers have developed a process known as backtesting. Backtesting refers to the practice in which a manager devises an investment strategy that he or she then tests using a computer, which shows how this strategy would have done, measured against historical rates of return, if it were used in the past. The manager adjusts this strategy until it shows the most favorable results, and then designs a "model portfolio" "that would have been 100% in cash during bad markets and 100% in other assets when they shone."[29]

But backtesting effectively creates a phantom record of excellent performance that is little more than the product of statistical manipulation with the benefit of hindsight, rather than accurate predictions based on solid historical evidence. There's a reason that backtesting is not permitted for regular mutual funds. As finance reporter Jason Zweig points out, "investing with someone solely on the basis of backtested results is like giving your money to a racetrack tout who can tell you who will win every race—but only after the horses cross the finish line."[30] This is precisely what occurred with American investment firm Niemann Capital Management, which advertised a risk-managed model ETF portfolio with an excellent return rate of 11.65% annually for the past five years, ending September 28, 2012. The only problem was that these portfolios weren't available to external clients until January 1, 2012, which meant that any favourable results measured prior to December 31, 2011 weren't actually earned by outside investors, but were simply the result of backtesting. To be fair, Niemann themselves point out in their disclosures that "the information given is historic and backtested and doesn't indicate actual past or future performance."[31] Yet how many investors were bilked into thinking that they could get such an extraordinary return from ETFs? Niemann's executives blame the consumer for not being educated enough to listen to reason;[32] however, most companies bury such disclosures in legalese and advertise backtested performance results to bait or mislead clients into using investment strategies that aren't suited for them.

In some cases, ETFs might be considered a sensible choice, especially for the average, low-risk investor who has neither the time nor the knowledge necessary to closely manage his or her own funds. However, one should always be aware that bankers count on their clients' lack of knowledge to charge more than they should be paying. Where ETFs are concerned, keep in mind that you should never pay more than 1.25% in total costs for an ETF. Always make sure you clearly know

- what the total cost for investing and building an ETF portfolio;
- when the firm was established that will run the portfolio;

- whether the disclosures of the ETF strategist comply with Global Investment Performance Standards set by the Certified Financial Analysts Institute;
- annual turnover rates;
- what proportion of the return on the ETF-managed portfolio in the prior year was taxable as short-term capital gains; and
- for those in the US, whether the portfolio invests in commodity ETFs that could require you to file K-1 tax forms, which could raise your accounting bills.[33]

Credit Cards

The last, but certainly not least, factor in how banks take advantage of their customers is through credit cards. Banks make money from credit cards because most major credit card organizations, like Visa and MasterCard, are linked with big banks. Likewise, most of the major Canadian and US banks are also credit card issuers: TD-Canada Trust, Royal Bank, CIBC, Scotiabank, Bank of America, HSBC, Chase, Citibank, and so on. The banking credit-card system first developed in the late 1970s and allowed for personal credit to expand from regional or local businesses to national, and eventually, international businesses. This innovation also introduced the option for customers to pay their balance in installments, which allowed the banks to collect interest on credit card purchases.[34]

Aside from collecting interest, the bank also collects revenue from multiple sources associated with credit card use. Every time a retailer accepts a credit card purchase, for example, they are required to pay a sales commission to the issuing bank. Likewise, because "the majority of credit card issuers' assets are accounts receivable," the banks can liquidate these assets "quickly to collection agencies to minimize default risk and quickly convert souring assets to cash."[35] For its part, the credit organization (e.g., Visa or MasterCard) makes its money from transaction fees that allow the banks to use their payment network: they move money around but don't extend credit or issue cards themselves. Since the banks take on the risk of the cardholder defaulting payment, they are also entitled to a bigger cut of the retailer and transaction fees. In essence, the credit organization serves as a middleman for banks to create additional revenue streams. This system has worked out remarkably well for the banks. According to journalist Gabriella Morrongiello, in 2010, the largest credit card issuers in the world—HSBC, Capital One, Citigroup, Chase, and Bank of America—made a combined profit of close to $3.85 billion, a good portion of which came from interest fees alone.[36]

As the system stands, debtors are at the mercy of creditors. In the US, three credit reporting agencies (Equifax, Transunion, and Experian) gather information about credit card users' spending habits, such as whether they hold revolving accounts and don't pay off their bills each month, how high their balances are on the cards they own, and so on. Fair Isaac then compiles the information to create a credit score, which determines how likely a consumer is to pay a bill. Lenders evaluate a consumer's risk to determine his or her interest rate using this credit score. Creditors can then change the terms of the credit card agreements with debtors if a credit score becomes lower or if a bill is paid late. That means that the interest rate a borrower was comfortable with for a purchase can be raised, making a purchase much more expensive than anticipated. Credit card fees are a source of huge profit for credit card companies, which charge even more for late payments or going over the credit limit.

Given that the average American family today carries upwards of six credit cards and carries over $7,000 in credit card debt,[37] and the average Canadian, though by and large more careful with their credit cards than Americans, held over $3,500 in credit card debt,[38] credit card interest rates and transaction fees should be a concern. In truth, most consumers don't have the time or the inclination to become experts in personal finance. Mandatory regulations, rather than merely a voluntary code of conduct, are necessary and need to be imposed on creditors to provide consumers with a fighting chance. It's easy to be ignorant about how much a purchase will cost with interest if only minimum payments (which often barely cover the interest amount) are made. Many people with unrealistic ideas about how long it will take to pay off their debts worsen the situation if they continue to rely on credit as they make their payments.

Conversely, how many people wrap consumer debt into their mortgages because the interest rate is lower? This thoughtless debt shift adds years to the life of a mortgage, eats into a homeowner's equity, and piles thousands of dollars of interest onto the home loan because it is so large and takes a longer time to pay off. But in the credit game, the worst culprits are payday loan services, which have some of the highest interest rates and prey upon those living paycheck to paycheck who are unable to make their budgets balance. Big banks own many payday loan companies, and payday loans bring in big profits. For example, payday loan company Advance America charges a $102.27 fee for a $500 loan in Texas, and the loans must be paid off on the following payday. That makes the annual interest rate 533.30%.

According to the credit card documentary *Maxed Out*, "the average American household . . . spends more than $1,300 a year in interest payments." One of the film's interviewees—Harvard Law professor Elizabeth Warren—states, distressingly, that credit card companies prey upon those who have claimed bankruptcy because they have "a taste for credit," meaning "they are willing to make minimum payments forever."[39] Given the high interest rates associated with credit card debt, we can see how this type of strategy would be extremely lucrative for credit card companies. To make matters worse, if users ever make a late payment they are hit with a penalty fee and their interest rate will be raised.

As long as creditors are able to increase interest rates by even 2% or 3%, borrowers will be at extreme risk of losing everything. We need to encourage people to pay down debts, and to empower them by making debt repayment less daunting. We also need to return to a culture of saving, a point I make again in the chapter on culture. Unfortunately, inflation plays a key role in hindering that goal. If inflation is high and money doesn't appear to be holding onto its value, people are less likely to save. But saving money truly improves a person's standard of living. Having savings to turn to makes it easier to avoid turning to creditors in times of need.

Key Takeaways

- Over the past thirty years, there has been a wide-scale movement towards bank deregulation.

- Over-deregulation can lead to a lack of transparency, irresponsible business practices, and exploitation of the free market at the expense of the public at large.

- Past and present scandals demonstrate that the banking industry is incapable of policing itself effectively.

- Derivatives trading have been a major factor in exacerbating the current crisis.

- ETFs can be a low-risk, low-cost investment, but beware of layered fees and skewed results from backtesting.

- The banks are making big money from your credit card debt.

- We ought to return to a culture of thrift and saving, so we rely less on credit cards when times are tough.

ENDNOTES

1 Alejandro Komai and Gary Richardson, "A Brief History of Regulations Regarding Financial Markets in the United States: 1789–2009," National Bureau of Economic Research, 2011. <http://www.nber.org/papers/w17443>

2 Ibid.

3 Ibid.

4 Ibid.

5 Ibid.

6 Ibid.

[7] Bert Ely, "Savings and Loan Crisis," *The Concise Encyclopedia of Economics*, 2nd ed, Library of Economics and Liberty, 2007. <http://www.econlib.org/library/Enc/SavingsandLoanCrisis.html>

[8] Financial Crisis Inquiry Commission, *The Financial Crisis Inquiry Report*, January 2011. <http://www.gpo.gov/fdsys/pkg/GPO-FCIC/pdf/GPO-FCIC.pdf>

[9] Greenspan qtd. in *Financial Crisis Inquiry Report*, January 2011.

[10] Financial Crisis Inquiry Commission, January 2011.

[11] Ibid.

[12] Ely, 2007.

[13] *New York Times*, "Times Topics: Charles H. Keating," N.d. <http://topics.nytimes.com/topics/reference/timestopics/people/k/charles_h_keating_jr/index.html>

[14] Financial Crisis Inquiry Commission, January 2011.

[15] Ibid.

[16] Bank for International Settlements, "International Regulatory Framework for Banks (Basel III)," 2012. <http://www.bis.org/bcbs/basel3.htm>

[17] Institute of International Finance, "Multiple Layers of Financial Regulatory Reforms Hold Back Economic Growth and Will Continue to Do so for Some Time," 6 September 2011. <http://www.iif.com/press/press+203.php>

[18] Dodd-Frank Wall Street Reform and Consumer Protection Act (Public Law 111-203) (US Government Printing Office), Approved 21 July 2010. <http://www.gpo.gov/fdsys/pkg/PLAW-111publ203/html/PLAW-111publ203.htm>

[19] Greg Smith, "Why I Am Leaving Goldman Sachs [Op-Ed]," *New York Times*, 14 March 2012. <http://www.nytimes.com/2012/03/14/opinion/why-i-am-leaving-goldman-sachs.html?pagewanted=all>

[20] US Securities and Exchange Commission, "Citigroup to Pay $285 Million to Settle SEC Charges . . . ," 19 October 2011. <http://www.sec.gov/news/press/2011/2011-214.htm>

[21] *The Economist*, "Exchange-Traded Funds: From Vanilla to Rocky Road [Special Report]," 25 February 2012. <http://www.economist.com/node/21547989>

[22] Jason Zweig, "When Cheap Funds Cost Too Much," *Wall Street Journal*, 15 October 2012. <http://online.wsj.com/article/SB10000872396390444657804578050501097576018.html>

[23] Brooke Masters, "Exchange Traded Funds Could Be Victims of Their Own Success," *Financial Times*, 13 October 2011. <http://www.ft.com/intl/cms/s/2/25bbd564-e82e-11e0-9fc7-00144feab49a.html#ixzz1bM6luPIq>

[24] Zweig, 15 October 2012.

[25] Masters, 13 October 2011.

[26] Ibid.

[27] Zweig, 15 October 2012.

[28] Ibid.

[29] Ibid.

[30] Ibid.

[31] Niemann disclosures qtd. in Zweig, 15 October 2012.

[32] Ibid.

[33] Ibid.

[34] *Encyclopaedia Britannica Online*, "Credit Card," N.d. <http://www.britannica.com/EBchecked/topic/142321/credit-card>

[35] David Ingram, "How Issuing Banks Benefit from Credit Cards," eHow.com., N.d. <http://www.ehow.com/facts_5873584_issuing-banks-benefit-credit-cards.html>

[36] Gabriella Morrongiello, "How Banks Make Money Off of Credit Cards," *The Daily Barometer*, 17 May 2012. <http://www.dailybarometer.com/news/how-banks-make-money-off-of-credit-cards-1.2872867#.UJ1Z1uOe_B5>

[37] Nerdwallet.com, "American Household Credit Card Debt Statistics Through 2012," 2012. <http://www.nerdwallet.com/blog/credit-card-data/average-credit-card-debt-household/>

[38] *Huffington Post*, "Average Canadian Household Debt Hits $112,329: BMO," 8 June 2012. <http://www.huffingtonpost.ca/2012/06/06/average-canadian-household-debt_n_1575172.html#slide=326454>

[39] *Maxed Out: Hard Times, Easy Credit, and the Era of the Predatory Lending*, Dir. James Schurlock, 2007.

PART TWO

Microeconomic Factors

Chapter Six

HOW YOUR PERSONALITY AFFECTS YOUR WEALTH

"If you don't know who you are, the market is an expensive place to find out." – Adam Smith

BENJAMIN FRANKLIN FAMOUSLY said that we can be sure of only two things in life, death and taxes. But there is at least one more thing that we can add to Franklin's list, and that's that our personality affects our investment behavior. Take Larry, for instance. As a high-powered CEO of a system engineering company, Larry is an alpha male who likes to be in control. Although he doesn't necessarily know a lot about investing, he likes to invest, especially in certain prestige companies and products, because it makes him feel powerful and important. But when evaluating an option, Larry sometimes tends to underestimate the risk and think he is right. Given Larry's dominant, demanding personality, is it any wonder he sometimes holds onto bad stock picks too long or tries to beat the market?

As Robert C. Doll, president and chief investment officer of Merrill Lynch makes clear: "In most human endeavors, individual psychology affects behavior and, ultimately, results. Anyone who has ever gone on a diet or started a workout regimen knows that. Investing is no different. Whether you're trying to shrink your waistline or grow your nest egg, discipline and self-awareness go a long way."[1] The good news is that understanding our personality traits can help increase our potential for financial success.

Our personality influences our attitudes, fears, and concerns; and the way we think, feel, and make decisions has a direct impact on our financial well-being. Over the past two decades, social scientists have been conducting research that predicts our economic behavior based on our personality.[2] Recent studies demonstrate that our personality affects how much we earn, save, or borrow, and, in the business world, how we finance our company's operations and growth.

Personality traits are relatively stable characteristics that cause us to behave in pretty much the same way over a lifetime. Most of us know people who are anxious, risk-takers, confident, or shy. Everyday language includes the use of thousands of such traits to help us better understand each other and how we will behave. While personality traits are difficult to change, there are coping strategies associated with different traits that can be managed for greater success. The key is to recognize whether a problem exists and then devise strategies to control or limit bad decisions.

That's why, just as I did in my first book, *The Greatest Enemy Is You*, I describe five of the most common personality types that influence how people make decisions about their finances. Only this time I expand and refine the descriptions to help you better understand the connection between particular personalities and the behavior patterns to which they give rise. I also add the personality of the more successful individual money manager as a model on which you can base your own behavior. The idea here is to raise your awareness so that you're able to make more educated decisions with your money.

The Procrastinator

Gary, a dynamic chef who had his own cooking show and a signature restaurant, suddenly died of an undiagnosed medical condition when he was in his mid-forties. Despite a $5 million estate and many potential heirs, Gary, like many investors in their forties, had neglected to draft a will. A reluctance to deal with the idea of dying, especially when it seemed so far away, led him to put off the stress of preparing an estate plan. But because he died without one, his family had to wait an agonizing six years while the estate ground through probate court.

If this textbook case of procrastination sounds familiar, it's no wonder. According to Piers Steel, a University of Calgary professor in the Haskayne School of Business and a leading researcher on procrastination, "at least 95% of us procrastinate at least occasionally and about 15–20% of us do it consistently and problematically."[3]

We procrastinate when we delay an important task until tomorrow in spite of being aware that we will be worse off for the delay. Financial advisors like to demonstrate the high cost of procrastinating by showing the effects of waiting to invest in retirement. They show, for example, that a person who delays investing for retirement until forty years old misses out on the compound gains earned by someone who started saving at thirty. Thus, the forty-year-old will have to contribute more per year to have the same amount of money by the time they both reach sixty-five.

Table 6–1: A Comparison of Two Investors

	Investor A	Investor B
Age at which person started investing	30	40
Number of years investing	35	25
Annual investment	$2,000	$4,062
Rate of return	6%	6%
Total amount invested	$70,000	$101,550
Total value of investment	$222,870	$222,870

So why does procrastination occur?

Researchers who study procrastination have discovered two psychological biases that account for why we procrastinate. The first refers to the timing of rewards and punishments or, more specifically, our preference for immediate rewards and punishments rather than those in the distant future (e.g., retirement). It turns out that we prefer doing those things that offer some kind of reward now, even though these things may hurt us in the long term. For example, a CBC news report on retirement savings among Canadians says that, in 2010, only 26% of eligible Canadians made contributions to RRSPs.[4] The report, which is based on figures from Statistics Canada, also shows that Canadian taxpayers have accumulated about $632 billion in unused RRSP contribution room—money that could be collecting investment returns to fund their future retirement.

The second bias related to procrastination is known as "task aversion." Put simply, the more frustrating or boring a task is, the more likely we are going to avoid doing it. As evidence, Steel cites a survey by H&R

Block indicating that "procrastinating on taxes costs people on average $400 because of rushing and consequent errors, resulting in over $473 million in overpayments in 2002."[5]

While no one is immune to psychological biases, the person who procrastinates is more susceptible to them than others. That's because the person who procrastinates tends to be impulsive, easily distracted, and lacking in self-control. Not surprisingly, researchers have also found that people lacking self-control dislike financial planning.

So what can be done about procrastination? The first step is simple self-awareness. As Tim Pychyl, a director of the Procrastination Research Group at Carleton University in Ottawa, explains: "There is no secret ingredient, no magic route to self-change—Just you developing personal insight into how you undermine your own goal pursuit."[6]

But personal insight isn't enough on its own; you also need to take concrete actions to avoid becoming a procrastinator (or else you might procrastinate on not becoming a procrastinator). Some of these actions could include

- developing a plan for completing tasks that you don't like or don't find meaningful such as filing your taxes;
- setting aside a specific time and location for your financial decision-making where there are no distractions or other demands; and
- giving yourself financial deadlines (e.g., aiming to save a certain amount of money by the end of the year).

With a little structure and willpower, your ability to resist the temptation to put off until tomorrow what can be done today will improve, just like a muscle that gets stronger over time with exercise.

The Know-It-All

We've all had run-ins with people who think they know everything there is to know about anything worth knowing. Disagreeably arrogant, know-it-alls think they're smarter or more skilled than the rest of us, and they're not afraid to let us know. In their need to be seen as experts, know-it-alls monopolize conversations, dismissing the opinions, comments, or suggestions of others. Although know-it-alls spend a great deal of time and energy analyzing information and building their knowledge, they lack the ability to admit when they're wrong or when they don't know enough to form an opinion. In other words, know-it-alls have a deeply rooted overconfidence in their beliefs and judgments.

But overconfidence can distort decision-making. And when it comes to financial decision-making, the failure to recognize the limits of their knowledge and skills puts know-it-alls at an even greater disadvantage. Ask any financial advisor and they'll tell you that "no matter how well educated or intelligent you are, it's hard to make financial decisions that are unbiased and in line with your interests."[7] Yet know-it-alls often don't see that what they don't know about things like compound interest, inflation, and risk diversification has an impact on their retirement wealth and investment behavior. Academics, for example, find that overconfidence leads individual investors to "overestimate their knowledge, underestimate risks, and exaggerate their ability to control events."[8] The result is under-diversified portfolios, bad investments, and more frequent trading since know-it-alls think they know the best time to buy and sell. The research, however, says otherwise. When it comes to investing, overconfidence reduces wealth.[9]

Always remember that good decision-making requires an understanding of the limits of your knowledge. One of the most important lessons that the ancient Greek philosopher Socrates used to teach his students was that the beginning of knowledge is knowing that you don't know it all. The same advice applies here: don't assume that you're already an expert when it comes to managing your personal finances. To help you guard against overconfidence, here are a few suggestions for becoming a more effective decision-maker:

- Continue to develop your financial knowledge.
- Always develop an investment plan before you invest.
- Try to identify some of the factors that point to success for an investment, rather than explaining it by your ability to trade effectively. Develop realistic expectations by studying historical returns of specific investments and asset classes. Research will reveal that certain investments can potentially offer higher returns because they carry more risk.
- Rebalance your portfolio at least once a year to ensure that your portfolio allocation reflects your investment objectives and risk profiles.
- Define and incorporate an appropriate amount of risk within your investments.
- Don't neglect the wisdom of other people.

The Nervous Nellie

If you're a nervous Nellie, you're more likely to experience stress and intense emotions in the face of uncertainty. Such a strong, negative reaction to stress makes it difficult to think clearly and make decisions, two qualities necessary for making sound financial choices. In fact, when it comes to market investing, nervous Nellies just aren't very comfortable with anything they might or might not do. They fear the loss of their money more than they desire investment gains, and so have little stomach to bear risk. As a result, they may not enter the market at all or, if they do, they'll invest only in very low-risk, low-return investments.

But in avoiding greater risk, nervous Nellies may not generate the returns they need to meet such goals as being able to retire comfortably at age sixty-five. And if nervous Nellies do decide to take a chance on higher risk, higher return investments, they will most likely abandon them when market conditions are poor. Author Rich Willis describes a nervous Nellie's reaction to the declining stock market of 2008 and

2009 in his book *Cognitive Investing*.[10] Out of anxiety, she sold her stocks in February 2009, the bottom of the decline, only to miss out as they recovered in value the next year. The lesson for nervous Nellies is clear: while you might miss some bad moments in the market by selling holdings when they decline in price, you are also likely to miss the upswings.

The first step to becoming a more effective investor should be listening to your financial planner. In its annual survey of investor behavior, the financial services market research firm Dalbar found that those investors who succumbed to their fears in the face of the stock market ups and downs of 2011 decided to take their losses instead of risking further declines, despite the advice of their financial planners. As a result, "equity investors lost 5.73% in their flight to safety compared to the gain of 2.12% that simply holding to the S&P 500 produced."[11] It's also important to use self-control strategies, such as checks, barriers, and rules, to prevent knee-jerk reactions to bad news or market fluctuations. As trading coach Brett Steenbarger says in summarizing the findings of a personality test administered to 64 traders, "'success in trading is related to the ability to stay consistent and plan-driven'."[12]

Other strategies include

- learning to notice and take cues from your emotional reactions and not dwelling on past losses;
- when noticing your emotions, avoiding putting any value judgment on them, since these judgments can give rise to further reactions (annoyance, disgust, anger, frustration, self-congratulation);
- avoiding information about how the market or your portfolio is performing in order to stick to your long-term investment strategy;
- developing an exit plan before entering investment positions; and
- considering an automatic investment strategy, such as dollar-cost averaging, investing the same amount at regular intervals.

The People Pleaser

It's hard not to like the people pleaser. Trusting, sensitive, and concerned about the welfare of others, the people pleaser wants friendly, harmonious relations above all else. In their striving to please others and seek their approval, people pleasers simplify problems and minimize anything upsetting. Because they are giving, they have difficulty saying "no," which is hard on a budget. People pleasers are also easily overwhelmed by financial information and rely heavily on the advice and opinions of others, which leaves them open to bad decisions or even fraud. For this reason, they might also believe the government will take care of them through social security and retirement homes even if they have no retirement assets.

Being over-friendly and likeable has other costs as well. Researchers have found that, compared to others, people pleasers have less savings, more debt,[13] and lower wages.[14] In other words, they have less wealth than others, perhaps because being too nice "works against savings or high-return investing."[15] Trusting or following what others say or do when investing, people pleasers sell on dips and buy when a stock is rising and, as a result, report larger peak losses. A study led by Jeremy Bernerth, assistant professor at Louisiana State University's E. J. Ourso College of Business, also noticed that people pleasers have lower credit scores.[16]

To account for the surprising finding, Bernerth told *Time* magazine that "people who want to get along with everyone and make others happy might be more likely to bend to sales pressure to apply for store credit cards."[17] He also speculated that people pleasers "might be more easily persuaded to make unwise financial decisions on behalf of financially irresponsible loved ones, like co-signing a loan or a credit card."[18] Whatever the reason, it's hard not to conclude that nice guys (and girls) need help getting their finances in order. Here are some suggestions that people pleasers would be well advised to follow:

- Learn to think a little differently and detach yourself from the crowd.

- When making a financial decision, weigh the influence of social norms and peer pressure.
- Create a new budget with dedicated savings for your goals.

The Dreamer

Ahh, the dreamer. Sitting at his desk daydreaming about his hoped-for promotion or the lottery winnings that will put an end to his financial woes. Dreamers are into wishful thinking and magical solutions, which can make them impulse spenders who have difficulty following a budget. Even if dreamers are trying to save, they often end up with a lot of credit card debt. They are too ready to borrow because they are too optimistic about their ability to repay. They tend to have big goals for the future with few plans for making them happen, clinging to beliefs like "my kids will take care of me when I am old." Some of their goals and plans can be wildly unrealistic given their financial standing.

When it comes to investing, the advantage goes to the realists, who sell to dreamers and buy from nervous Nellies. Unrealistic optimism can wreak havoc on investment portfolios and financial security. Dreamers think short term and trade a few stocks frequently based on little information. They may diversify too little, trade too much, and trust luck to bail them out. They often have a penchant for risk-taking, which they find stimulating. In addition, they see money as a vehicle for obtaining freedom, excitement, and less stress in life. They set up businesses without realistically factoring in their chance of failure.

Dreamers need self-control strategies to overcome their tendency to be impulsive and superstitious. At the very least, they need a financial advisor to help them identify sound, reachable goals. When it comes to investing, they should

- select investments based on strategic planning and in-depth research, not emotions or hot tips; and

- establish clearly defined, realistic investment objectives in terms of return requirements and risk tolerance.

The Disciplined Investor

We can learn how to improve our own financial decision-making and investment behavior by more closely modeling ourselves on what I call the disciplined investor. Disciplined investors are hardworking, organized, and dependable.[19] Their self-discipline and ability to delay gratification enables them to stick to a budget and savings plan in the face of immediate temptation. Thus, they save more and spend less than others. One study found that disciplined investors were three times more likely than others to be regular savers who saved on average 10% to 12% of their income.[20] Disciplined investors also have higher lifetime earnings.[21] When it comes to market investing, they are humble (not overconfident), flexible, comfortable with change, and emotionally resilient. According to Steenbarger, the personality traits of the disciplined investor are "the most reliable predictor of trading success."[22]

Thomas J. Stanley reported similar findings in his book *The Millionaire Mind*. During in-depth interviews with several successful millionaires, Stanley identified the factors considered vital to the millionaires in achieving their financial success. These included self-discipline or self control in every area of their life, hard work, and frugality.[23] For a picture of who such a disciplined millionaire might be we need look no further than businessman and investor Warren Buffet. The media reports, for example, that "[a]side from an addiction to luxury air travel," Buffet is "a man of simple tastes and frugal habits."[24] Despite a fortune worth $44 billion,[25] Buffet remains uninterested in accumulating the trappings of wealth, pays close attention to ongoing expenses, and lives in the same Omaha, Nebraska, house that he bought in 1958 for $31,500.[26] During an interview with CNBC, he advised young people to "'stay away from credit cards.' Paying interest on credit cards not only suggests that you are living beyond your means, but it also means that you are losing money."[27]

A Common Theme

The personalities profiled here clearly drive behaviors and decisions in different ways. That's why understanding your particular personality will help you avoid the most common pitfalls affecting such things as your risk tolerance, composure, and desire for financial discipline. At the same time, however, the importance of self-awareness and self-control cannot be overstated.

Self-awareness, the capacity to recognize your emotions and how they affect your thoughts and behavior, and self-control, the ability to control impulsive feelings and behaviors, are critical to your financial success. Being able to manage your emotions will enable you to invest, save, and borrow better than those who are overpowered by their emotional reactions. By using the personality profiles here as a guide in developing greater self-awareness and self-control, you will be better able to patiently and slowly build wealth over the long term.

Key Takeaways

- Personality traits are difficult to change, so devise mechanisms to control or limit bad decisions.

- Procrastinators delay important tasks until tomorrow in spite of being aware that they will be worse-off for the delay.

- The main reasons we procrastinate are our preference for immediate rewards rather than those in the distant future, and the desire to avoid frustrating or boring tasks.

- Know-it-alls have too much confidence in their beliefs and judgements, and overconfidence can distort decision-making.

- Nervous Nellies aren't comfortable investing because they're afraid of losing their money and have little tolerance for risk.

- Investing only in low-risk, low-return investments does not generate the returns needed for goals such as retirement.

- People pleasers have fewer savings, more debt, and lower wages. They also have lower credit scores.

- Dreamers need self-control strategies to overcome their tendency to be impulsive and superstitious. A financial advisor will help dreamers identify sound, reachable goals.

- Disciplined investors are hardworking, organized, and dependable; they are also self-disciplined and have the ability to delay gratification.

- Warren Buffet is a good example of a disciplined investor. His advice to young people is "stay away from credit cards'."

ENDNOTES

1 Doll qtd. in "The Key to Reducing Investing Mistakes: Understand Your Investing Personality," *Journal of Financial Planning*, January 2005. <http://www.fpanet.org/journal/BetweentheIssues/LastMonth/Articles/TheKeytoReducingInvestingMistakesUnderstandYourInv/>

2 Ellen K. Nyhus, Empar Pons, and Paul Webley, "Personality and Economic Behavior," *Advances in Psychology Research*, Vol. 18, ed. by Serge P. Shohov (New York: Nova Science, 2002).

3 Piers Steel, "Measure My Procrastination!" *The Procrastination Equation*, N.d. <http://procrastinus.com/the-procrastinus-survey/>

4 CBC, "Retirement Savings in Canada—By the Numbers," 29 February 2012. <http://www.cbc.ca/news/business/taxseason/story/2012/02/21/f-rrsp-retirement-planning-numbers.html>

5 Piers Steel, "The Nature of Procrastination: A Meta-Analytic and Theoretical Review of Quintessential Self-Regulatory Failure," *Psychological Bulletin*, Vol. 133, No. 1 (2007).

6 Tim Pychyl, "Procrastination Therapy: The Secret Ingredient for Success," Don't Delay blog, *Psychology Today*, 1 April 2009. <http://www.psychologytoday.com/blog/dont-delay/200904/procrastination-therapy-the-secret-ingredient-success>

7 Centre for Policy Development, "Understanding Human Behavior in Financial Decision-Making: Some Insights from Behavioral Economics Centre," Paper presented by Ian McAuley at the No Interest Loans Scheme Conference, Australia, June 2009.

8 Stéphane Robin and Katerina Stránická, "Personality Characteristics and Asset Market Behavior," Paper presented at the 29th Journées de Microéconomie Appliquée, Brest, 7–8 June 2012.

9 Ibid.

10 Rich Willis, *Cognitive Investing: The Key to Making Better Investment Decisions* (AuthorHouse, 2011).

11 Dalbar, *2012 Quantitative Analysis of Investor Behavior*, Advisor Ed, April 2012.

12 Steenbarger qtd. in "Affect and Financial Decision-Making: How Neuroscience Can Inform Market Participants," by Richard L. Peterson and Camelia M. Kuhnen, *Journal of Behavioral Finance*, Vol. 8, No. 2 (2007).

[13] Ellen K. Nyhus and Paul Webley, "The Role of Personality in Household Saving and Borrowing Behavior," *European Journal of Personality*, Vol. 15 (2001).

[14] Ellen K. Nyhus and Empar Pons, "The Effects of Personality on Earnings," *Journal of Economic Psychology*, Vol. 26 (2005).

[15] Angela Lee Duckworth and David R. Weir, "Personality, Lifetime Earnings, and Retirement Wealth," Working Paper 2010-235, University of Michigan Retirement Research Center, October 2010.

[16] Bernerth cited in "Nice Guys' Credit Scores Finish Last," by Martha C. White, *Time*, 7 November 2011.
<http://moneyland.time.com/2011/11/07/nice-guys-credit-scores-finish-last/>

[17] Ibid.

[18] Ibid.

[19] Duckworth and Weir, October 2010.

[20] Nyhus and Webley, 2001.

[21] Ibid.

[22] Steenbarger cited in Peterson and Kuhnen, 12 August 2005.

[23] Stanley cited in *Finding Financial Freedom: The Biblical Road to Wealth*, by Grant R. Jeffrey, 20 August 2005.
<http://www.grantjeffrey.com/pdf/freedom_intro_cap1_2.pdf>

[24] Anthony Bianco, "The Warren Buffett You Don't Know," *Bloomberg Businessweek*, 4 July 1999.
<http://www.businessweek.com/1999/99_27/b3636001.htm>

[25] *Forbes*, "Warren Buffet," March 2012.
<http://www.forbes.com/profile/warren-buffett/>

[26] CNBC cited in "Warren Buffett's Frugal, So Why Aren't You?" by Lisa Smith, *Investopedia*, 5 January 2010.
<http://www.investopedia.com/articles/financialcareers/10/buffett-frugal.asp>

[27] Ibid.

Chapter Seven

CAN CULTURE INFLUENCE YOUR FINANCIAL DECISIONS?

"Culture is a little like dropping an Alka-Seltzer into a glass—you don't see it, but somehow it does something." – Hans Magnus Enzensberger

WHETHER YOU LIVE in Canada or the US, chances are you put a premium on individual freedom and, with it, the virtues of self-reliance and personal responsibility. To a greater or lesser degree, you believe that success is primarily the result of your own initiative and hard work. But the belief that we are completely self-made neglects at least one factor that lies outside our control, even though, like a powerful magnet, it pulls our behavior in a particular direction. That factor is culture, the set of shared values, beliefs, and underlying assumptions that a particular group or society transmits from generation to generation.

To be fair, it's easy to overlook the influence of culture. Culture is like an iceberg: the tip that sits above the water line—the outward behaviors and practices characteristic of a group, such as dress, food, manners, laws, and language—makes up just a small part of a larger whole. The larger, submerged part of the iceberg comprises the internal beliefs, values, attitudes, and expectations that determine our view of reality and how we behave. These core values and ideas are acquired, consciously and unconsciously, through imitation and interactions with parents, teachers, neighbors, religious teachings, officials, the organizations we join, the media, and society-at-large. As a result, we internalize a culture's basic assumptions and beliefs so that they operate in us without our conscious awareness and outside our conscious control. Like water to fish, we live within our culture without knowing that it exists or how it influences our actions and attitudes. But if we fail to realize that our assumptions and beliefs are learned ideas, not necessarily a reflection of things as they are, we tend to regard our viewpoints as unfailingly right, as a reflection of the natural order of reality. In short, unless we work at becoming conscious of our culture's influence on us, we risk becoming narrow-minded, stubborn, and righteous.

Not surprisingly, acting out our hidden or implicit assumptions leads us to judge others from the standpoint of our values. This, in turn, generates arguments and misunderstandings in our personal lives, and reverberates in our collective lives. As an example, Americans, steeped in the culture of individualism, "tend to believe that the poor could become rich if they just tried hard enough,"[1] while Europeans, with their long history of class distinctions and inherited wealth, "blame contextual factors like luck or social and economic conditions."[2] Both groups believe that they are right; neither recognizes that they are viewing the world through the filter of a particular culture. But because of the belief that success is a matter of effort, US governments favor less income redistribution and government intervention than European governments, although as economists Alberto Alesina and George-Marios Angeletos point out, in trying to make economic outcomes more fair, the European approach actually "distorts market allocations, increases the effect of luck, and makes economic outcomes unfair."[3]

What about the way that cultural values are expressed in our financial behavior? The fact is, we rely on our culture's common store of knowledge to make decisions about how we save, spend, and invest. As a result, the tendency to act out our cultural values and biases can have significant financial implications, such as low savings and high consumption. Thus, cultural self-awareness is a key to success in managing debt and building credit, accumulating and protecting assets, and preparing for retirement.

You may have trouble believing that financial decisions are often based on invisible cultural factors. In beginning to see the roots of your attitudes and behavior regarding money in your own culture, you will become better able to change your behavior. Self-reflection is a necessary part of this growing awareness. As you read about the extent to which culture shapes our financial lives, I encourage you to think about the influence of your own family and your family's religious and ethnic roots on your attitudes about money. Most importantly, I hope that you'll open your mind to the possibility that you have a culture and that you cannot hold yourself apart from its influence. Your financial health depends on it.

The Influence of Ethnicity

Not everyone finds it easy to save money. For a number of reasons— from a staggering burden of debt to ignorance about savings options to the temptation to spend on the array of gadgets and goods available in stores—some people fail to sock away money for a rainy day or their retirement. However, studies reveal yet one more barrier to making good financial decisions, namely, that the cultural assumptions and values of your ethnic group or race can influence your financial decisions without you knowing it or understanding why.

Two recent surveys on financial behavior make just that point. The first, a study released in February 2012 by the ING Retirement Research Institute, surveyed different ethnic groups, including African-Americans, Asians, and Hispanics, to understand their attitudes and behaviors regarding retirement. The results suggest that "distinct cultural differences" affect some groups more than others when it comes to planning and saving, whether for an emergency or retirement.[4]

These differences were especially evident in the finding that nearly half of Hispanics (47%) and half of African-Americans (50%) have one month or less saved for emergencies compared to just one-in-four Asians. Hispanics also think about retirement goals less than any other group and have the lowest average balance in employer-sponsored retirement plans ($54,000 vs. the $69,000 average balance for all groups). Asians, meanwhile, had the highest average plan balances at $81,000. A senior manager at ING US explained Hispanics' disinclination to focus on retirement goals by noting that the importance of family, a strong cultural value, affects the choices they make about their finances: "many times in the Hispanic community, parents will sacrifice their own financial future in order for their children to advance."[5]

The second survey by Prudential Financial echoed the results of the ING study, even though it zeroed in on the financial behavior of women. It found, for example, that Hispanic women had the lowest median savings, $10,400 vs. $12,400, among respondents, while Asian women had the highest median savings ($58,600). The survey also confirmed that the majority of Hispanic women (73%) identified taking care of their parents and immediate family as important.[6] These differences among cultural groups led a panel of Prudential economists to conclude that "racial/cultural influences play a key role in determining how women approach financial security and planning."[7]

Not only are Hispanics and African-Americans less likely than Asians to save for an emergency or retirement, they are also less likely than Whites to own stocks, bonds, or mutual funds. According to the authors of a study on investor risk tolerance, different "cultural values" among Whites enables them to accept greater risk and a possible loss in their investment portfolio better than members of non-White minority groups.[8] This suggests that non-Whites prefer low-risk investments, such as savings accounts, time deposits, and life insurance, those that are less likely to result in a loss but that tend to provide lower rates of return and generate wealth more slowly.

Research on the wealth held by African-American, Hispanic, and White households seems to bear this out. Economist Sharmila Choudhury shows that, while differences in home equity become smaller between Whites and other ethnic groups the higher their income, the differences in ownership of financial assets becomes greater, especially in "riskier, higher-yielding assets."[9] In other words, no matter the level of income or education, African-Americans and Hispanics in the US are less likely than Whites to have a well-diversified investment portfolio that includes high-risk financial assets such as stocks and corporate bonds. The result is that White households are "far wealthier,"[10] and getting more so since the economic downturn of 2008.[11]

Why this might be so can be explained by a number of factors, including limited access to investment options and a preoccupation with near-term events, like making a large purchase or saving for college, rather than distant events, such as saving for retirement.[12] Still, these explanations don't get at the root of the matter, namely, that underlying any financial decisions are the values, norms, and knowledge related to financial management that we acquire largely in childhood from our families.[13]

A study by the FINRA Investor Education Foundation, confirming that parents are the "main source" of the financial knowledge of minority communities, in fact reminds us that much of what we know about saving, spending, and borrowing comes from our parents, much of it the result of their behavior and the family's level of financial security. For instance, the FINRA study found that the parents of Asians were more likely to discuss "the importance of saving money for the future."[14] And as we've seen from the ING Retirement Research Institute and the Prudential Financial studies previously mentioned, the Asian adults who were surveyed fared the best when it came to their level of savings. In other words, for those who want to change the destiny of their racial or ethnic group, a good place to start is in the home during childhood.

Men Are from Mars, Women from Venus

Of course, ethnicity is not alone in molding an individual's cultural profile and hence influencing savings behavior. A well-documented body of research shows that men and women also approach financial decisions from vastly different perspectives. For example, compared to men, women feel far less confident about insurance issues and financial, investment, and tax planning.[15] Women also tend to be more cautious and less willing to tolerate risk when making investment decisions, and they are less likely to invest regularly, use an investment strategy, or regularly "review and compare their investment performance with market benchmarks."[16] The Prudential study mentioned earlier found that, the majority of female respondents (70%) "see themselves as savers rather than investors."[17]

A report by Vanguard Group, Inc., an international investment management company, demonstrates the truth of women's self-assessment with its finding that more women than men in the same income range ($30,000 to $100,000) join work-sponsored retirement plans and contribute more.[18] Yet, because women tend to have lower lifetime earnings, their "absolute savings" is lower than that of men.[19] Their lower savings, coupled with the fact that women tend to live longer than men, suggests the need for women to focus on strategies to build retirement wealth and to respond to poorly performing investments.

Religion as an Element of Culture

If you don't consider yourself religious, it may be a revelation to learn that religion also has an impact on savings and investment decisions and, hence, an individual's financial wealth. Like the values and beliefs associated with your ethnic or racial group, the influence of religion on your behavior is due in part to the effect of religious beliefs on your parents' money management practices, as well as others who form a part of their social network.[20] But religion also has a more indirect or circuitous effect on our level of wealth. That's because religious values influence the behaviors that affect individual wealth, including education, marriage, divorce, and the decisions to have children, the number of children to have, and whether the mother will stay at home or go out to work.[21] Thus, differences in the beliefs and practices of religious denominations can result in differences in individual and household wealth.

A study on the connection between religion and wealth, for example, looked at "conservative" and "mainline" Protestants, Catholics, Jews, and non-religious individuals in the US.[22] Jews were found to be the wealthiest group both because their religion does not emphasize the afterlife—instead promoting worldly pursuits such as educational achievement, career success, and the accumulation of wealth—and also because the history of the Jewish *diaspora* has encouraged them to invest in financial assets rather than fixed assets. As a result, the median net worth of Jews was $150,890, three times larger than the $48,200 of the full sample. In addition, 56% of Jews owned stocks compared to 24% of all respondents.

At the other end of the scale, however, were conservative Protestants with a median net worth of just $26,200. Unlike Jews, only a small proportion of conservative Protestants owned their own home, invested in stocks, or inherited any wealth. The study's author attributed these disparities in wealth to the traditional beliefs of conservative Protestants. Because of these beliefs, conservative Protestants tend to have bigger families, to home-school their children, and to save less for education. In addition, fewer women work outside the home. With less wealth, children growing up in these homes are less likely to learn the behaviors for successful saving and investing or to come into contact with the people who can model different financial behavior.[23]

On the plus side, however, all religions promote values that affect savings decisions. Research demonstrates that since all the major religions encourage hard work, thrift, individual responsibility, and honesty while discouraging debt and poverty,[24] religious people are more likely than non-religious people to save money[25] and teach their children the importance of thrift.[26] As the authors of a study on the role of religion in household finance in the Netherlands put it, "religious individuals care significantly more about thrift."[27] In spite of an emphasis on frugality, however, certain religious beliefs also encourage caution and risk aversion, which, in turn, can lead to investment in lower risk, lower return assets, and, as a result, a lower level of total wealth. The point to take from this discussion is the need to question your assumptions and habits to ensure they are not hurting your efforts to accumulate wealth.

National Character

As we've seen, religion generally encourages thrift. And, from a household to a nation, research indicates that a sense of thrift can have a positive impact on national savings rates.[28] Moreover, household savings are the main source of domestic funds for capital investment in business expansion, factories, technology, and so on. Religious values also contribute to other attitudes conducive to national prosperity, including trust in others, the government, and the law.[29] Without these attitudes, there is greater willingness to, for example, accept or pay a bribe or cheat on taxes, and less likelihood of becoming an entrepreneur, sharing information, lowering transaction costs between trading partners, or attracting foreign investment. Religion, in other words, can contribute greatly, though indirectly, to the wealth of a nation, not just an individual. Indeed, a country's dominant religion, along with the personality characteristics typical of its adult citizens, its political system, and its major institutions combine to form a type of national character or culture by which a country is known.

The idea that a nation's culture and the attitudes to which it gives rise could drive the success of a national economy probably first gained credence with the French social thinker Alexis de Tocqueville. After a nine-month sojourn in America in 1831, he wrote *Democracy in America*, a study of the life and institutions of the country. There, de Tocqueville identified the "common set of civic virtues," including "hard work . . . thrift, integrity, self-reliance, and modesty," that grew out of the religion of Americans and contributed to the country's success as a democracy and free market economy.[30] The German sociologist Max Weber gave this idea further credence when he "dubbed the qualities that Tocqueville observed, the Protestant ethic and considered them the cornerstone of successful capitalism."[31] Historian David Landes revisited the idea in his 1998 book *The Wealth and Poverty of Nations*, arguing that, until non-industrialized countries internalize the cultural values of "thrift, hard work, tenacity, honesty, and tolerance,"[32] they will remain as economic backwaters. More recently, scholars confirm that the extent to which individuals favor competition, are not subject to force, see themselves as having control over their life, trust others, have a strong work ethic, and value thrift and honesty influences "economic policies, either directly or indirectly through better functioning institutions."[33]

Yet while these explanations explain the economic progress of western countries like the US and Canada, a look at the savings and consumption rates in both countries suggest that a countervailing force may be undermining traditional values. For example, while countries such as Taiwan, Hong Kong, Singapore, and China boast high household savings,[34] the US and Canada—with the exception of a reversal in 2009 not projected to last[35]—have seen steady declines since about the mid-1990s.[36] The flip side of the 2009 savings rates of 4.3% in the US and 5% in Canada means that North Americans are spending an astronomical 95% of their after-tax income.[37] which leaves them unprepared for any unexpected change in their living situation, such as the loss of a job, medical emergency, or expensive car repairs.

Naturally, as savings have declined, consumption of goods and services has steadily increased. In Canada, for example, per capita personal consumption amounted to $24,952 (2002 dollars) in 2010, a 68% jump from its 1981 level of $14,849.[38] In the US, personal consumption of goods and services in 2010 totaled about $10.2 trillion, or 70.5% of GDP.[39] Jörg Mayer, a senior economist at the United Nations Conference on Trade and Development, notes that, since the late 1990s, the increase in personal consumption by Americans has been due largely to debt financing, not a rise in income.[40] Authors Eric Olin Wright and Joel Rogers illustrate the effect of consumer spending in their critique of American society by noting that, "[f]rom the 1960s until the early 1980s, the median size of a new home in the United

States varied up and down around 1,500 square feet."[41] Today, over 40% of new houses are larger than 2,500 square feet, despite having fewer people per household on average. As one scribe writes, compared to 50 years ago, "Americans today own twice as many cars per person, eat out twice as often and enjoy endless other commodities that weren't around then—big-screen TVs, microwave ovens, SUVs and handheld wireless devices, to name a few."[42]

So what does this suggest is happening in the US and Canada? Why the shift from saving to spending and still more spending? What happened to the Protestant ethic and with it the willingness to defer gratification? The answer, at least in part, is a rapidly growing consumerist culture that emerged during the economic boom of the 1920s with the development of mass production, new technologies, and advertising, and continued to grow and spread to what it is today—a society in which consumerism has become a voracious but insatiable monster.

The Rise of Consumerism

That's right. An ever-expanding culture of consumerism is eroding traditional cultural values and exerting enormous pressure to spend and consume. Instead of devoting our time and energy to work and frugality, we now devote it to spending and getting, believing that personal happiness can be found through buying and owning things. Shopping has become a recreational activity, and we spend a lot of our time in shopping malls.[43] Every day the media bombards us with advertising encouraging us to buy as a means to achieve the good life and social status. And because credit is widely available, we borrow money now and pay later, sometimes revolving a balance month to month and paying interest on the outstanding amount.

But if you think you can simply escape the pressure to consume, think again. The forces promoting consumerism are legion. Economists encourage consumer spending because they regard it as the engine of economic growth and job creation. In the wake of the terrorist attacks of September 2001, for example, government leaders in Canada, the US, and Britain, fearful of recession, called on their citizens to do their patriotic duty and spend money.[44] In the economic crisis that began in 2008, the media warned that people needed to spend more and save less to enable the economy to recover.[45] But perhaps the most powerful and insidious force motivating us to buy is advertising.

Advertising pervades our lives: it appears on billboards, on cell phones, through direct mail, in magazines and newspapers, and, of course, on television. Without realizing it, we see, on average, 52,500 commercials a year on television;[46] the average child watches about 40,000 television commercials a year.[47] Young children are in fact ideal targets for advertising messages since they remember the ads they see and prefer the products displayed.[48] But advertising images and messages are displaying and reinforcing certain values about personal happiness and social success. As Wright and Rogers explain, advertising exerts its influence by "constantly affirming the association between happiness and consumption, between success in life and buying things, between sexual attractiveness and particular forms of consumption."[49] Advertising images and messages become part of the "taken-for-granted culture" we learn from early childhood and that make "a life heavily oriented to consumption seem natural."[50]

But advertising also fosters a culture of instant gratification. Not only do we want to buy, but we want to buy now. So instead of saving and waiting until we have enough to buy what we see advertised, we have credit cards that make it possible to buy now and pay later. Ever since 1959 and the option to "revolve" a credit card balance from month to month became available,[51] credit card use and credit card debt has been growing. From 1980 to 2008, credit card debt in the US nearly tripled to $2.56 trillion.[52] By June 2012, the average American household owed $7,271 in credit card debt.[53] That figure was $3,709 for Canadians in 2011.[54] In addition, a 2011 survey by the Strategic Counsel found that 36% of Canadians and half of Americans do not pay their balance off in full every month.[55]

The good news is that a movement to return to earlier values and change the habit of overspending is dawning. For example, in 2012, the American Savings Education Council and the Consumer Federation of America came together to make February 19 to 26 "America Saves Week" as a way "to promote sensible savings habits that last year-round."[56] The Center for Thrift and Generosity, which had its start in 2005, has a similar mandate to establish thrift—"a time-honored idea that Benjamin Franklin once championed"[57]—as a meaningful way of life. More recently in Canada, the CEO of the Canadian Imperial Bank of Commerce, speaking to senior government officials and business leaders at a National Summit on Pension Reform, proposed enabling Canadians to make voluntary contributions to the Canada Pension Plan as a way to "'reignite a culture of savings'."[58] In a speech to the Economic Club of Canada, the CEO of AGF Management Ltd., an investment management firm, suggested making savings compulsory, as is the case in Singapore, where workers must save 25% of their salary, and their employers must match 10% of it. It's too early to see where these proposals will go. In the meantime, however, we would do well to recognize the need to take action when it comes to resisting appeals to spend.

What You Can Do

So what can you do to counteract the influence of cultural values that might lead to unwise financial decisions? The key to transforming self-defeating financial behaviors is to deepen self-understanding and appreciation for the complexity of your situation. With increased understanding and self-awareness, commitment to changing cultural values around spending and saving will begin from within, the only place from where such change can start. Here are few tips to get you started:

- Become mindful of your values, the ideals with which you orient your life.

- Recognize the need to return to a culture of saving and thrift.
- Learn to look at your own culture from an outsider's perspective.
- Think about what went on in your childhood when it came to your allowance, discussions about money, the purchases you made, and purchases that were made for you.
- Become aware of what motivates you to buy and save and invest the way you do.
- Before your next purchase, ask yourself why you want to buy the item, notice how you made your spending decision, and consider whether your decision-making approach is helping or hurting you.
- Set weekly limits on how much TV your family will watch and stick to them.

Key Takeaways

- Culture is the set of shared values, beliefs, and underlying assumptions that a particular group or society transmits from generation to generation.

- "[D]istinct cultural differences" affect some ethnic groups more than others when it comes to planning and saving, whether for an emergency or retirement.

- African-Americans and Hispanics in the US are less likely than Whites to have a well-diversified investment portfolio that includes high-risk financial assets such as stocks and corporate bonds.

- Compared to men, women tend to be more cautious and less willing to tolerate risk when making investment decisions, and they are less likely to invest regularly, use an investment strategy, or regularly "review and compare their investment performance with market benchmarks."

- Since all the major religions encourage hard work, thrift, individual responsibility, and honesty while discouraging debt and poverty, religious people are more likely than non-religious people to save money and teach their children the importance of thrift.

- The extent to which individuals favor competition, are not subject to force, see themselves as having control over their life, trust others, have a strong work ethic, and value thrift and honesty influences "economic policies, either directly or indirectly through better functioning institutions."

- The US and Canada—with the exception of a reversal in 2009 not projected to last—have seen steady declines in household savings rates since about the mid-1990s.

- A culture of consumerism is eroding traditional cultural values and exerting enormous pressure to spend and consume.

ENDNOTES

[1] Alberto Alesina and George-Marios Angeletos, "Fairness and Redistribution: US versus Europe," Discussed at Macroeconomics and Individual Decision Making Conference, 1 November 2003.
<http://aida.wss.yale.edu/~shiller/behmacro/2003-11/alesina-angeletos.pdf >

[2] Gizem Arikan, "Economic Individualism and Government Spending," World Values Research, Vol. 4, No. 3 (2011).

[3] Alesina and Angeletos, October 2002.

[4] ING, "ING Study: Cultural Influences Impact Retirement Planning and Decision Making," 2 February 2012. <http://ing.us/about-ing/newsroom/press-releases/ing-study-cultural-influences-impact-retirement-planning-and-decis>

[5] Ibid.

[6] Prudential Financial, *Financial Experience and Behaviors Among Women: 2012–2013 Prudential Research Study*, 2012.
<http://www.prudential.com/media/managed/Pru_Women_Study.pdf>

[7] DiversityInc, "Diversity Management: Turn Women's Financial Concerns into Measurable Gains," 25 July 2012.
<http://www.diversityinc.com/diversity-management/diversity-management-turn-womens-financial-concerns-into-measurable-gains/>

[8] John E. Grable and Ruth H. Lytton, "Investor Risk Tolerance: Testing the Efficacy of Demographics as Differentiating and Classifying Factors," Association for Financial Counseling and Planning Education, 1998.

[9] Sharmila Choudhury, "Racial and Ethnic Differences in Wealth and Asset Choice," *Social Security Bulletin*, Vol. 64, No. 4 (2001/2002).

[10] Ibid.

[11] Tami Luhby, "Worsening Wealth Inequality by Race," CNN Money, 21 June 2012.
<http://money.cnn.com/2012/06/21/news/economy/wealth-gap-race/index.htm>

[12] D. Anthony Plath and Thomas H. Stevenson, "Financial Services and the African-American Market: What Every Financial Planner Should Know," *Financial Service Review*, Vol. 94 (2000).

[13] Sharon M. Danes, "Parental Perceptions of Children's Financial Socialization," *Financial Counseling and Planning*, Vol. 5 (1994).

[14] FINRA Investor Education Foundation, *Exploring the Investment Behavior of Minorities in America*, 2007. <http://www.finrafoundation.org/web/groups/foundation/@foundation/documents/foundation/p118420.pdf>

[15] Ruthie Ackerman, "Caution Can Work to Women's Advantage," *InvestmentNews*, 8 April 2012. <http://www.investmentnews.com/article/20120408/REG/304089965>

[16] FINRA Investor Education Foundation, *Examining the Investment Behavior of High Income Women in America*, 2007. <http://www.finrafoundation.org/web/groups/foundation/@foundation/documents/foundation/p118418.pdf>

[17] Prudential Financial, 2012.

[18] Luhby, 21 June 2012.

[19] Ibid.

[20] Lisa A. Keister, "Religion and Wealth: The Role of Religious Affiliation and Participation in Early Adult Asset Accumulation," *Social Forces*, Vol. 82, No. 1 (September 2003).

[21] Ibid.

[22] Ibid.

[23] Ibid.

[24] Rachel M. McCleary, "Salvation, Damnation, and Economic Incentives," *Journal of Contemporary Religion*, Vol. 22, No. 1 (January 2007).

[25] Anja Klaubert, "Striving for Savings: Religion and Individual Economic Behavio," University of Lüneburg, Working Paper Series in Economics, No. 162 (January 2010). <http://www.leuphana.de/fileadmin/user_upload/Forschungseinrichtungen/ifvwl/WorkingPapers/wp_162_Upload.pdf>

[26] Luigi Guiso, Paola Sapienza, and Luigi Zingales, "Does Culture Affect Economic Outcomes?" *Journal of Economic Perspectives*, Vol. 20 (January 2006).

[27] Luc Renneboog and Christophe Spaenjers, "Where Angels Fear to Trade: The Role of Religion in Household Finance," Tilburg University, No. 2009–34, May 2009.

[28] Guiso, Sapienza, and Zingales, January 2006.

[29] Luigi Guiso, Paola Sapienza, and Luigi Zingales, "People's Opium? Religion and Economic Attitudes," *Journal of Monetary Economics*, Vol. 50 (2003).

[30] Tocqueville cited in Steven Malanga, "Whatever Happened to the Work Ethic?" *City Journal*, Vol. 19, No.3 (Summer 2009).

[31] Ibid.

[32] Landes qtd. in Guiso, Sapienza, and Zingales, January 2006.

[33] Sascha Buetzer, Christina Jordan, and Livio Stracca, "Euro Area Imbalances: A Matter of Culture?" Paper presented at The Eighteenth Dubrovnik Economic Conference, 27–29 June 2012.

[34] Juann H. Hung and Rong Qian, "Why Is China's Saving Rate So High? A Comparative Study of Cross-Country Panel Data," Congressional Budget Office, Working Paper 2010-07, 8 July 2010.

[35] Organisation of Economic Co-operation, "Household Saving Rates Forecasts," 7 June 2012. <http://www.oecd-ilibrary.org/economics/household-saving-rates-forecasts_2074384x-table7>

[36] Valentina Pasquali and Tina Aridas, "Household Saving Rates," Global Finance, November 2012. <http://www.gfmag.com/tools/global-database/economic-data/12065-household-saving-rates.html>

[37] Ibid.

[38] Centre for the Study of Living Standards, *Beyond GDP: Measuring Economic Well-being in Canada*, September 2011. <http://www.csls.ca/reports/csls2011-11.pdf>

[39] Kathryn J. Byun and Christopher Frey, "The U.S. Economy in 2020: Recovery in Uncertain Times," *Monthly Labor Review*, Vol. 135, No. 1 (January 2012).

[40] Jörg Mayer, "Global Rebalancing: Effects on Trade Flows and Employment," United Nations Conference on Trade and Development Discussion Paper, No. 200, September 2010.

[41] Eric Olin Wright and Joel Rogers, *American Society: How It Really Works* (W.W. Norton, 2010).

[42] Tori DeAngelis, "Consumerism and Its Discontents," *Monitor on Psychology*, Vol. 35, No. 6 (June 2004).

[43] Michael Guiry and Richard J. Lutz, "Recreational Shopper Identity: Implications of Recreational Shopping for Consumer Self-Definition," Working paper, University of Florida, May 2000.

[44] Jill Vardy and Chris Wattie, "Shopping Is Patriotic, Leaders Say," *National Post*, 28 September 2001. <http://www.commondreams.org/headlines01/0929-04.htm>

[45] *Newsweek*, "Stop Saving Now!" 13 March 2009. <http://www.thedailybeast.com/newsweek/2009/03/14/stop-saving-now.html>

[46] Wright and Rogers, 2010.

[47] American Psychological Association, "Television Advertising Leads to Unhealthy Habits in Children; Says APA Task Force," 23 February 2004. <http://www.apa.org/news/press/releases/2004/02/children-ads.aspx>

[48] Ibid.

[49] Wright and Rogers, 2010.

[50] Ibid.

[51] Barbara O'Neil, "Cultural Differences in Handling Credit," eXtension, 26 September 2011. <http://www.extension.org/pages/25269/cultural-differences-in-handling-credit>

[52] Malanga, Summer 2009.

[53] NerdWallet, "American Household Credit Card Debt Statistics Through 2012," N.d. <http://www.nerdwallet.com/blog/credit-card-data/average-credit-card-debt-household/>

[54] Doug Hoyes, "Massive Credit Card Debt Leads to Bankruptcy in Canada," Bankruptcy Canada, 28 February 2011. <http://www.bankruptcy-canada.ca/trustees-talk/bankruptcy-canada/20110228/bankruptcy-canada-credit-card-joe-debtor.html>

[55] Canadian Bankers' Association, "Credit Cards: Statistics and Facts," 27 September 2012. <http://www.cba.ca/en/media-room/50-backgrounders-on-banking-issues/123-credit-cards>

[56] Brad Tuttle, "Why You're Supposed to Be Extra Focused on Saving Money This Week," *Time*, 22 February 2012. <http://business.time.com/2012/02/22/why-youre-supposed-to-be-extra-focused-on-saving-money-this-week/>

[57] William Mattox, "Forgetting Our Frugal Roots," *USA Today*, 13 August 2012. <http://usatoday30.usatoday.com/news/opinion/forum/story/2012-08-13/thrify-ben-franklin-frugal/57039184/1>

[58] Barbara Shecter, "CIBC Set to 'Reignite a Culture of Savings'," *Ottawa Citizen*, 21 February 2013. <http://www.ottawacitizen.com/business/CIBC+reignite+culture+savings/7994008/story.html>

Chapter Eight

THE SURPRISING TRUTH ABOUT HOW WE MAKE DECISIONS

"The investor's chief problem—and even his worst enemy—is likely to be himself." – Benjamin Graham

IF YOU'VE ALWAYS thought of yourself as a pretty level-headed decision-maker, you may feel offended to learn that we don't always make financial decisions on the basis of rationality alone. These days, a new field of experimental research dubbed behavioral finance or behavioral economics is challenging the notion, long standard in traditional economic theory, that we are rational decision-makers, able to access and assess all available information, and interested only in maximizing gain over time. By applying insights from psychology to understand the behavior of people as they make financial decisions and their subsequent effect on markets, behavioral finance demonstrates that we often act in seemingly irrational ways, making decisions based on gut feelings and intuition rather than reason alone.

The implications of the tendency to act irrationally show up in a range of financial situations, from investing to choosing credit cards to planning about if, how, and when to save for retirement. For example, Robert Shiller in his book *Irrational Exuberance* shows that "investors usually rely on wishful thinking, others' opinions, or hearsay for their information."[1] Researchers have found that people make "financial mistakes" in dealing with credit card fees and interest payments on home equity loans, mortgage loans, and car loans.[2] And as for the failure of many North Americans to plan or save enough for retirement, well, I've already discussed the issue in the chapters on personality and culture. Suffice it to say that the accelerating trend toward defined contribution plans places responsibility for managing retirement savings squarely on the shoulders of individuals, not organizations. This is both liberating and alarming since, as Kent State University professor Paul J. Albanese concludes, "the economic assumption of rationality is violated in the behavior of every person."[3]

But the good news is that the decision errors we make are predictable. In its quest to identify and learn how we actually make decisions, as opposed to how we have been theorized to do so, behavioral finance has discovered that we tend to make the same types of "systematic and predictable judgment errors"[4] over and over again and in the same situations: when, for example, making decisions in the face of uncertainty, estimating the statistical likelihood of events, and trading off costs and benefits that will be realized at different times. If all this sounds a little abstract, it might help to know that these systematic decision errors occur when we need to decide whether to invest in a safe money market account or a volatile stock, or choose whether to invest in a savings plan or buy a big-screen TV.

The point is that, because these errors of decision and judgment fall into distinct patterns, we can learn to identify them and hopefully avoid making them in the future. I say hopefully because even Daniel Kahneman, one of the early pioneers to explore the irrational ways we make decisions, famously admitted his own inability to completely avoid the decision errors to which we are prone. Still, in his book *Thinking, Fast and Slow* he emphasizes the importance of becoming aware of how we think and the biases to which we fall heir, as well as the need to approach important decisions, such as how much money to save for retirement, from whom to buy a mortgage, or whether and when to simplify and consolidate investments, deliberately and thoroughly. In this chapter I therefore set out to help you understand why you make the financial decisions you make and how you can try to correct the irrational elements of these decisions. By doing so, I hope to help you do what so many find difficult: adhere to a disciplined investment plan so that you can achieve your long-term financial goals. To do that, we need first to understand a little about what accounts for these decision errors.

How Our Brain Works

According to the economic theory of utility (e.g., well-being, benefit, satisfaction), people make decisions among alternatives based on their preferences, choosing the option that represents the highest personal or *utility* value through a rational decision-making process. That is, we "first map out all the alternatives, find the possible outcomes of each of them, estimate the probability for each of these outcomes, . . . calculate the expected utility of each alternative, and finally select the alternative with the highest expected utility."[5] In contrast to the theory of utility, however, Herbert Simon, a Nobel Prize winner in economics, claims that we opt to expend the least required effort to get a good-enough result rather than the best possible alternative. As Simon puts it, "'[h]owever adaptive the behaviour of organisms in learning and choice situations, this adaptiveness falls far short of the ideal of maximizing in economic theory. Evidently, organisms adapt well enough to 'satisfice'; they do not, in general, optimize'."[6]

Since Simon's insight into what he termed "bounded rationality"—the notion that we neither have access nor the ability to process all the information we need when making decisions[7]—psychologists have identified two main ways our brains reason and make decisions: System 1 and System 2 thinking. System 1 thinking is automatic, fast, emotional, effortless, uncontrolled, and unconscious.[8] In contrast, System 2 thinking is reflective, more effortful, controlled, deductive, slow, and conscious.[9] System 2 can also override or possibly correct

System 1 thinking if the stakes are high enough.[10] We typically rely on System 1 thinking in situations of "bounded rationality," that is, when we don't have the time or ability to carefully process all of the available information. However, research suggests that, because it's easier and faster, we mostly operate in System 1.[11]

The problem, of course, is that System 1 thinking can lead to those systematic errors in judgment and decision I've already mentioned. These types of errors occur because System 1 processes information through mental shortcuts and emotional filters known as behavioral or psychological biases.[12] Experts suggest that these biases are hard-wired into our brains[13] and, for the most part, they lead to good results. But psychological biases also predispose us to look at things in a way that inhibits logical thinking. For example, Kahneman, also a Nobel Prize winner in economics, notes that we're biased to believe as true a statement we hear frequently than one we don't hear as often.[14] These psychological biases fall into two broad categories: cognitive and emotional, which we'll now explore.

How We Think

Cognitive biases distort the way we see reality. They include basic statistical and memory errors common to us all, regardless of how smart, rich, or educated we are. Since the introduction of bounded rationality in the 1950s,[15] research into judgment and decision-making has accelerated and, consequently, expanded the list of cognitive biases. This ever-growing list can be categorized in a number of ways. But here we'll look at just two factors responsible for producing erroneous beliefs: the first is motivational and the second is cognitive.

Self-Deception Errors

Self-deception errors reflect the fact that we are motivated to protect our self-image and self-confidence. We see what we want to see and so we mislead ourselves into believing claims about ourselves even when they are false. For example, almost all of us believe that we are smarter and more tolerant than the average person—even though this is statistically impossible. As Thomas Gilovich points out in his book *How We Know What Isn't So*, 70% of senior high school students thought they were above average in leadership ability, and only 2% thought they were below average.[16] Nor was the inclination to think highly of oneself limited to young students. A survey of university professors found that 94% thought they were better at their jobs than their average colleague.[17] Given how extensive self-deception appears to be, see if you can recognize yourself in these two examples of self-serving biases:

- **Confirmation bias:** A confirmation bias is the tendency to seek out evidence that confirms our beliefs while ignoring or discounting as irrelevant information that contradicts our beliefs. Such selective thinking leads us to alter our perceptions to make it appear as though what we see validates an established decision. Gilovich suggests that we put greater weight on information that confirms our position because it's easier to understand and deal with than it is to try and figure out the information that would go against our position.[18] But the consequences of confirmation bias can lead us to find, for example, information that proves an investment decision was the right one, while overlooking risks or information that would question the wisdom of the investment. In other words, the confirmation bias prevents us from looking strategically at an investment once we have already made it.

- **Self-attribution bias:** Because we want to feel good about our decisions, and ourselves, we tend to attribute success to ourselves and blame other people or other outside factors for our failures. In doing so, we overestimate our own abilities at the risk of overconfidence. Although we manage to keep our self-esteem intact, overconfidence, as we've seen from a previous chapter, can lead people to underestimate the risks such that they fail to invest adequately in insurance.[19] Overconfidence can also induce people to borrow more readily than they might otherwise because of an overly optimistic assessment of their ability to repay, or they might set up a business without taking a realistic view of their chances of failure.[20] The self-attribution bias also gets in the way of learning from past mistakes since we don't recognize them as our own or remember them.[21]

At this point, a word of caution seems in order. While it may be tempting to think we're too smart to fall for these kinds of biases, consider this: just as we tend to think we're above average, so do we tend to believe we are less susceptible than the majority of people to a whole host of these "judgmental biases."[22]

Heuristics

Heuristics (rules of thumb or intuition) refer to the second cognitive bias under review here. Heuristics exist because there are limits to the amount and complexity of information that we are able or willing to process. We often have to make decisions quickly even when we might not have all the information we need and while feeling tired or distracted. Faced with constraints on our mental capacity, our minds reach for shortcuts to simplify decision-making.[23] In many cases, these simple heuristics lead to decisions that are almost as good as those reached using the most rigorous logic and reasoning powers, and often require far less effort. But they don't always provide the right answer in every situation. In this section, I focus on several heuristics, or rules of thumb, that can lead to systematic errors in how we make financial decisions.

- **Availability:** Not only is our judgment affected by how often we encounter a piece of information, but also by how easy or difficult it is to remember it. Rather than examine other options, we tend to make judgments about the risk of an event or situation occurring based on how readily examples come to mind. If, as we make a decision, a number of relevant examples immediately spring to mind, we are far more likely to judge these events as being possible and to feel frightened and concerned. As researcher Melissa A. Z. Knoll suggests, people who hear frequent, or even one especially dramatic, news or dinner party story about other people losing their retirement savings may become nervous and "pull their money out of their retirement funds or shift their funds to less risky prospects."[24]

- **Status Quo Bias:** People have a strong tendency to stick with the status quo. Given a choice between doing something and doing nothing, we tend to do nothing. Economist Richard Thaler and legal scholar Cass Sunstein call the status quo bias "a fancy name for inertia" and identify "lack of attention" as one of its causes.[25] When faced with new options, we will often stick with the current state of affairs, for example, "to elect an incumbent to still another term in office, to purchase the same product brands, or to stay in the same job"[26] because it is easier. This tendency can work to our advantage in the case of automatic enrolment in employee savings plans since few of us will take action to exercise our right to opt out. But our preference for staying the course can negatively affect our investment decisions. For example, we may not periodically reallocate investment funds as market conditions change even when we are aware of recommended allocation strategies.

- **Loss Aversion:** Quite simply, people fear losing money. So much so, in fact, that researchers have found that we feel twice the pain from loss as we do from the pleasure of gain.[27] In the words of Kahneman and his frequent collaborator Amos Tversky, "losses loom larger than gains."[28] Aversion to loss means that we tend to seek risk when faced with possible losses and to avoid risk when a certain gain is possible.[29] Hence, when investing, we are more likely to sell winning investments too soon because we don't want to risk a loss, and to hang onto losing investments too long because we are willing to take a chance that the stock will go up again in value.[30]

  In addition, loss aversion can affect our inclination to save for retirement. Knoll reasons that, since people tend to use their take-home pay as their "reference point" for income, they will feel like they are losing spending money if they contribute to a retirement savings account.[31] Her recommendation is to set aside a portion of your earnings for automatic transfer into a retirement account so that you don't experience it as a loss. As the old saying goes, "what you don't know can't hurt you."

How We Feel

Our emotions can also influence our financial decisions, in part because emotions are triggered by our beliefs, are experienced along a continuum of pleasure and pain, and are needed to drive our actions.[32] Hence, emotions play a role in driving us to seek pleasure and avoid pain. Moreover, because emotions are accompanied by "physiological arousal" (e.g., rapid breathing, sweating, muscle tension),[33] the force of strongly felt emotions, such as anger, fear, or euphoria, can overpower rational decisions and leads us to misunderstand situations and make errors in decision-making. For example, in *Irrational Exuberance*, Shiller points out that that the enthusiasm and greed of investors with their expectations for further price increases was "one of the most important factors" behind the bull market of 1983 to 2000, when asset prices rose to unsupportable levels.[34] In addition, the "brain stores emotional memories of past decisions," which the brain then refers to when interpreting and reacting to new events.[35] But these memories can mislead us, resulting in poor judgment and worse decisions. Here, then, are just a few of the emotional biases that color our choices.

Fear and Greed

This isn't rocket science. People are occasionally gripped by fear or overcome by greed. Brain scans show that the lure of making money stimulates the release of the same levels of dopamine, a neurotransmitter activated when something good unexpectedly happens, as when a cocaine addict anticipates his or her next hit.[36] Similarly, the possibility of losing money "activates the same fight-or-flight response as a physical attack, releasing adrenaline and cortisol into the bloodstream, resulting in elevated heart rate, blood pressure, and alertness."[37] Fear and greed are clearly powerful motivating forces that can get in the way of sensible decision-making. For example, "extreme fear . . . can cause investors to quickly sell all their risky assets at fire-sale prices in favor of government bonds and cash, which may not serve their longer-term objectives if they maintain these holdings for too long."[38] The greed of investors, on the other hand, moves stocks beyond their actual value. Andrew Lo, from the MIT Sloan School of Management, suggests that the cycle of fear and greed accounts for financial crises.[39] For example, in a bull market like that described by Shiller, greed leads to excessive leverage and unsustainable asset prices. In turn, the "inevitable collapse" of such a speculative bubble results in "unbridled fear, which must subside before any recovery is possible."[40] Contrary to the dictum that "greed is good" famously espoused by Gordon Gekko in Oliver Stone's 1987 film *Wall Street*, greed is not so good at all.

Hyperbolic Discounting

A fancy name for a common phenomenon, hyperbolic discounting refers to our tendency to prefer smaller payoffs now rather than larger ones later. Essentially, we discount options that promise a future reward when it requires sacrifices in the present, and then often regret our choices when the future arrives. That's because people tend to choose options that provide immediate gains over options that provide long-term benefits. This tendency to discount consequences that occur later in time has obvious application in "health outcomes, consumption choices over time, and personal finance decisions."[41] In fact, "[h]yperbolic discounting has been linked to the problems of addiction and self-control,"[42] which no doubt has an impact on our rising health care costs. Self-control likewise factors into decisions about retirement savings. Knoll likens it to going on a diet to lose weight: the decision to forego that tempting dessert for the sake of "future weight loss is similar to reducing one's current income (thereby forfeiting some tempting purchases) in the pursuit of a comfortable retirement."[43] Similarly, the chronic spender who carries "large credit-card debts at a high interest rate and [is building] pre-retirement wealth at a lower interest rate [displays a preference] for the rewards provided by buying something today [over] the discounted displeasure of future payments."[44] As Thaler and Sunstein wisely explain, "problems arise where people must make decisions that test their capacity for self-control."[45]

Addressing Your Biases

Perhaps the first thing you need realize is that psychological biases are here to stay. They evolved as adaptive traits to help human beings survive, and, as such, are innate, hard-wired in our brain. Hence, the first step to managing our biases is becoming aware of them and the problems they can cause. You can also mitigate their influence and improve your decision-making with the following approaches:

- Recognize and accept that emotional biases, such as greed, fear, regret, denial, anger, overconfidence, and a preference for good news, are as present in your investment decisions as they are in other areas of your life.
- Watch your greed and fear when it arises to become familiar with what triggers it. By understanding your triggers, you can use awareness of your emotional state to more easily recognize potentially difficult decisions when they arise.
- Create a written investment plan that describes your reasons for investing, your long-term goals, types of investments, and investment management strategies that will define your portfolio.
- Get information from many sources. Ask for feedback to determine whether your decision seems reasonable. Pay attention to those assessments that run contrary to your own judgments.
- Be humble about the complexity of what you are dealing with. To the greatest extent possible, test hypotheses on a small scale, where being wrong has less negative impact.

While becoming more analytical and incorporating factual information into your decision-making can help control the impact of biases, we cannot eliminate their influence. Ultimately, enlisting the help of an experienced financial advisor in your financial decision-making processes may be your best bet to ensuring you do not fall victim to psychological biases. A professional financial advisor can give you an objective perspective on your financial decisions and determine which strategies will work best for you and your situation.

Key Takeaways

- Behavioral finance demonstrates that we often act in seemingly irrational ways, making decisions based on our feelings and intuition rather than reason alone.

- We have two main ways our brains reason and make decisions: System 1 and System 2 thinking.

- System 1 processes information through mental shortcuts and emotional filters known as behavioral or "psychological biases."

- Self-deception errors reflect the fact that we are motivated to protect our self-image and self-confidence.

- A confirmation bias is the tendency to seek out evidence that confirms our beliefs while ignoring or discounting as irrelevant information that contradicts our beliefs.

- The cycle of fear and greed accounts for financial crises.

- Hyperbolic discounting refers to our tendency to prefer smaller payoffs now rather than larger ones later.

- The help of an experienced financial advisor is our best bet to ensuring we do not fall victim to psychological biases.

ENDNOTES

[1] Harlan Green, "The Pitfalls of Private Investing: Irrational Economic Behavior," *Popular Economics*, 25 April 2005.
<http://www.populareconomics.com/documents/FF/FF4-25-05.pdf>

[2] Sumit Agarwal, John C. Driscoll, Xavier Gabaix, and David Laibson, "Financial Mistakes over the Life Cycle," Paper presented at the SITE 2006 Summer Workshop, Psychology and Economics 6.0, Stanford University, 7–9 August 2006.

[3] Piers Steel and Cornelius J. König, "Integrating Theories of Motivation," *Academy of Management Review*, Vol. 31, No. 4 (2006).

[4] Melissa A. Z. Knoll, "The Role of Behavioral Economics and Behavioral Decision Making in Americans' Retirement Savings Decisions," *Social Security Bulletin*, Vol. 70, No. 4 (2010).

[5] Geir Kirkebøen, "Decision Behavior: Improving Expert Judgement," In *Making Essential Choices with Scant Information: Front-End Decision Making in Major Projects* (Palgrave MacMillan, Chippenham and Eastbourne, 2009).

[6] Simon qtd. in Kirkebøen, 2009.

[7] Kirkebøen, 2009.

[8] Keith Frankish, "Systems and Levels: Dual-System Theories and the Personal–Subpersonal Distinction," In *Two Minds: Dual Processes and Beyond* (Oxford University Press, 2009).

[9] Ibid.

[10] Knoll, 2010.

[11] Ibid.

[12] John Nofsinger, *The Psychology of Investing*, 3rd ed. (Prentice Hall: 2007).

[13] Dan Ariely, "Visual Illusions and Decision Illusions," Blog, 10 December 2009.
<http://danariely.com/2009/12/10/visual-illusions-and-decision-illusions/>

[14] Kahneman cited in "Storytelling Our Energy Future," by Chris Nelder, The Energy Futurist blog, smartplanet, 30 May 2012. <http://www.smartplanet.com/blog/energy-futurist/storytelling-our-energy-future/500>

[15] Kirkebøen, 2009.

[16] Thomas Gilovich, *How We Know What Isn't So: The Fallibility of Human Reason in Everyday Life* (The Free Press, 1991).

[17] Ibid.

[18] Gilovich, 1991.

[19] Aparna Dalal and Jonathan Morduch, "The Psychology Of Microinsurance: Small Changes Can Make a Surprising Difference," Microinsurance Paper No.5, International Labor Organization, September 2010.

[20] David de Meza, Bernd Irlenbusch, and Diane Reyniers, *Financial Capability: A Behavioral Economics Perspective*, Financial Services Authority, July 2008.

[21] Tristan Nguyen and Alexander Schuessler, "Investment Decisions and Socio-demographic Characteristics: Empirical Evidence from Germany," *International Journal of Economics and Finance*, Vol. 4, No. 9 (2009).

[22] Daniel Gilbert, "I'm O.K., You're Biased," *New York Times*, 16 April 2006. <http://www.nytimes.com/2006/04/16/opinion/16gilbert.html?pagewanted=1&ei=5090&en=673c17e958023fd3&ex=1302840000&partner=rssuserland&emc=rss>

[23] Nofsinger, 2007.

[24] Knoll, 2010.

[25] Richard H. Thaler and Cass R. Sunstein, *Nudge: Improving Decisions about Health, Wealth and Happiness* (Yale University Press, 2008).

[26] William Samuelson and Richard Zeckhauser, "Status Quo Bias in Decision Making," *Journal of Risk and Uncertainty*, No. 1. (1988). <http://dtserv2.compsy.uni jena.de/__c125757b00364c53.nsf/0/f0cc3cae039c8b4 2c125757b00473c77/$file/samuelson_zeckhauser_1988.pdf>

[27] Knoll, 2010.

[28] Daniel Kahneman and Amos Tversky, "Choices, Values, and Frames," *American Psychologist*, Vol. 39, No. 4 (1984).

[29] Brad M. Barber and Terrance Odean, "The Courage of Misguided Convictions," Association for Investment Management and Research, 1999.

[30] William N. Goetzmann and Massimo Massa, "Disposition Matters: Volume, Volatility and Price Impact of a Behavioral Bias," Yale ICF Working Paper No. 03-01, 28 January 2003.

[31] Knoll, 2010.

[32] Lucy F. Ackert, Bryan K. Church, and Richard Deaves, "Emotion and Financial Markets," *Economic Review*, Vol. 88, No. 2 (2003).

[33] Ibid.

[34] Shiller qtd. in Ackert, Church, and Deaves, 2003.

[35] Dan Vergano, "Study: Emotion Rules the Brain's Decisions," *USA Today*, 8 June 2006. <http://usatoday30.usatoday.com/tech/science/discoveries/2006-08-06-brain-study_x.htm>

[36] Andrew W. Lo, "Fear, Greed, and Financial Crises: A Cognitive Neurosciences Perspective," 12 October 2011.
<http://www.argentumlux.org/documents/Lo__2011__-_Fear__Greed__and_the_Financial_Crisis-_A_Cognitive_Neurosciences_Perspective.pdf>

[37] Ibid.

[38] Ibid.

[39] Ibid.

[40] Ibid.

[41] BehaviorLab.org, "Hyperbolic Discounting," N.d. <http://www.behaviorlab.org/Papers/Hyperbolic.pdf>

[42] Ibid.

[43] Knoll, 2010.

[44] BehaviorLab.org, N.d.

[45] Thaler and Sunstein, 2008.

Chapter Nine

THE WORST MISTAKES INVESTORS MAKE

"There is a genius on one side of every trade and a dolt on the other, but which is which does not become clear until much later." – Leo Levy

LEGEND HAS IT that Joseph Kennedy Sr., father of former US president John Kennedy, got out of the stock market before the crash of 1929 when he got stock tips from a shoeshine boy. He figured that if shoeshine boys have tips, the market's obviously too hot for its own good. An expert in dealing in the stock market of the day, Kennedy understood what many failed to notice, namely, that excessively high levels of investor optimism are a danger sign of "overvalued, overbought, overbullish"[1] conditions that are usually followed by a stock market decline. He also recognized that the best way to spot investor euphoria is when ordinary individuals jump into the market.

It turns out that Kennedy's intuition and good timing proved him right. In 1929, a rising bull market had convinced many, including then-president Herbert Hoover, that the stock market would continue to rise indefinitely.[2] A Yale University economist, Irving Fisher, famously proclaimed shortly before the 1929 crash: "'Stock prices have reached what looks like a permanently high plateau'."[3] At the time Fisher was making his prediction, the Dow Jones Industrial Average had soared from about 60 in 1921 to its peak of 381.17 on September 3, 1929.[4]

Millions of "'ordinary Americans'" had begun investing in the stock market believing that they could become rich.[5] Loose stock market regulations led to rampant speculation as investors borrowed money from banks to buy stocks on margin, paying as little as 10% of the price of a stock.[6] But, as we know, the overvalued speculative bubble burst, and prices started dropping like stones while banks tried to collect on loans made to investors whose holdings were worth little.

If this scenario sounds familiar, it should. Despite the lessons of history, investors all over the world continue to make the same mistakes over and over again. Japan, for example, experienced a speculative bubble from 1984 to 1989 when stock market prices, together with land prices, tripled.[7] The bubble was fuelled by land speculation—the practice of holding land in expectation of gain or as a hedge against inflation—and "a Japanese corporate invention, known as 'zaitech,' or 'financial engineering,' by which speculation became an integral part of corporate earnings statements."[8] The bubble popped when, in May 1989, a worried Japanese government raised interest rates to slow down the "skyrocketing values of the Nikkei [Japan's stock exchange] and land valuations."[9] But the move caused stock prices to plummet instead. By the end of 1992, stock prices had dropped 57% from 1989 values, resulting in a cascade of bankruptcies and defaulted loans,[10] while economic growth ground to a near halt throughout the decade.[11]

Nor did Japan's experience prevent two more recent bubbles—in stocks in the 1990s and, as we've already discussed, in housing from 2001 to 2007. A wholly new and untapped market made possible by the advent of personal computers—and the Information Revolution they triggered—as well as the creation of the Internet, spurred the so-called dot-com bubble of the mid 1990s to 2000. Excited by the commercial possibilities of the "New Economy," investors in western nations embraced the mantra that the old rules no longer applied.[12] New companies, primarily financed by venture capital and Initial Public Offerings (IPOs) of stocks, seemed to spring up every day. Stock prices skyrocketed because investors wanted to get in on the next big thing, even though many of the new Internet companies didn't have a sound business plan. The NASDAQ composite index of technology and growth companies "went from just over 1,000 to over 5,000 between 1996 and 2000, rising over 80% in 1999 alone."[13] But following a massive sell-off of dot-com stocks in March 2000, the bubble burst and hundreds of Internet-based companies went bankrupt, unemployment numbers rose, and the western "economy slipped into a recession."[14]

The US housing crisis of 2001 to 2007 is yet another example of a speculative bubble. It was a time when builders and developers as well as ordinary families purchased houses to sell for a profit, leading international business editor Ambrose Evans-Pritchard to describe the buying frenzy as "the mother of all bubbles—in sheer volume, if not in degrees of speculative madness."[15] As I've already discussed, Americans, lulled by a belief that home prices never fall and lured by the promise of amassing wealth in the face of rising home prices, ignored the fact that virtually everyone was getting a mortgage, an example of which was the No Income, No Asset (NINA) limited-information home mortgage.[16] Without the need to qualify for mortgages, and fuelled by speculation that prices would continue to rise, housing demand exceeded supply. But by 2005, stories of, for example, waiters buying four houses on speculation began to emerge, a sign that the housing mania was turning.[17] As David Stiff, chief economist of a housing data company, told *Bloomberg Businessweek*, "'a significant portion of demand [that] is speculative . . . can evaporate very quickly'."[18] Sure enough, buoyant optimism gave way to bug-eyed fear as housing prices and sales volumes began to slide downwards and foreclosures, bankruptcies, and unemployment began to rise. The years of easy financing, low interest rates, and steeply rising housing prices were over.

What these and other cautionary tales about economic bubbles reveal is that investing is a difficult business, and speculative investing a recipe for disaster. Investors should make decisions based on information and analysis, not risky, speculative forecasts. Above all, investors should avoid the trap of believing that this particular time will be different. Bottom line: while there's no guarantee that the money you invest will grow, having a clear understanding of what you are doing with your money and doing your homework will help you succeed over the long run. Toward that end, I describe a few more of the worst mistakes investors typically make and provide the outline of what I hope will become your personal investing manifesto.

Following the Herd

In the examples of economic bubbles just described, we can notice a number of common themes. Perhaps the most prevalent, not only in bubbles, but also in other investment decisions is the tendency to follow the herd. As we saw, fear and greed prompt people to stampede after the crowd, investing in stocks when all of their friends, family, and the financial media are bullish, regardless of price. Not wanting to miss out, they invest in the latest trend or hot tip—based on the simple premise that the majority can't be wrong. They behave in a way contrary to what investment guru Warren Buffett advised when he told investors to "[b]e fearful when others are greedy, and be greedy when others are fearful."[19] But since most investors focus on following the majority instead, they often purchase stocks when they are at the top of the market and won't invest when stocks dip until the market shows sign of recovery.

The Lure of Gold

An obvious example is the age-old adage about investing in gold as a hedge against inflation and a bulwark against uncertainty, such as fears about government debt and deficits, war and social unrest, and inflation. But since jewelry accounts for about 78% of the use of gold,[20] investors can evaluate the underlying value of only a relatively small percentage of the gold that is used for industrial purposes (industry, medical, and dental). Hence, gold is less of an investment than a speculation that the price will go up. As a result, its price is "highly arbitrary and subject to wild swings based on investors' changing sentiments."[21] Over the past four years, for instance, gold prices more than doubled, from around $843 an ounce at the end of 2008 to nearly $1,800 an ounce at the start of October 2012,[22] yet people still eagerly purchased gold as they heard of others' past success. But if they would just pause long enough to take a good, hard look at the long-term view, they would clearly see that actual returns are minimal when adjusted for inflation. The following chart from Jeremy Siegel, the Russell E. Palmer Professor of Finance at the University of Pennsylvania's Wharton School, demonstrates that $1 invested in gold over 200 years ago would have remained fairly flat and today yielded a 0.7% real return after inflation. That's not very much. On the other hand, the chart also shows that stocks are where the money is, since, by far, they have "the biggest growth trajectory of any other asset, and represent the best option for preserving your purchasing power over time."[23]

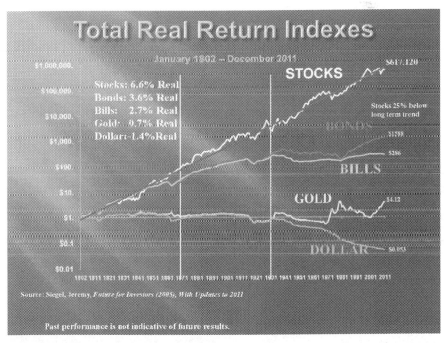

Figure 9–1: Total real return indexes, January 1802–December 2011

The Attraction of Foreign Currency

One of the most popular forms of trading these days is the opportunity to buy and sell foreign currency, which essentially involves buying the debt of foreign countries. Once limited to financial institutions and the super-rich, foreign exchange trading has become accessible to individual investors through exchange-traded mutual funds and bank certificates of deposit. A report from the Bank for International Settlements, for example, shows that the foreign exchange market grew by 20% from April 2007 to April 2010, with $4 trillion traded daily.[24] As a result, many experts are encouraging their clients to jump into the global currency trading market as a way to make money quickly and in less time. Even banks have been aggressively promoting foreign currency accounts as a way to diversify their clients' portfolios.[25] But if we recall what we've just learned about economic bubbles, we will know to approach any new, can't-lose megatrend with caution. Foreign exchange trading is no exception.

While advisors recognize that the foreign exchange market can be highly volatile, and hence risky, many still advocate investing in the currency of a foreign country with a stable economy as a sure thing. They mistakenly assume that the only research you need do is to look at the economic conditions of the country, such as GDP, employment levels, and so on. They don't consider taking into account what I refer to as "political will." Political will refers to the invisible force that motivates political action. The New York-based Charney Research firm defines political will as the combination of a large number of people holding strongly held opinions on polarizing public-policy issues.[26]

The effect of political will can be seen in the recent market interventions by two countries traditionally seen as homes to safe-haven currencies. Both the Bank of Japan and Swiss National Bank intervened to bring down the value of their currencies, which had been rising against the euro and US dollar because of a flurry of currency trading. In 2011, for example, the Swiss sent shock waves through the foreign exchange market when it pinned the exchange rate of its franc to the euro, essentially devaluing the franc by 8% to protect its economy.[27] The reason for doing so is that large migrations of excess capital, especially to a small country such as Japan or Switzerland, drives the value of a currency higher and consequently raises the price of that nation's exports, which, in turn, reduces its exports and economic growth. Hence, the decisions by governments in Japan, Switzerland, South Korea, and Taiwan to lower their exchange rates and boost their competitiveness. Even business-friendly Singapore has been issuing warnings about the strength of its currency.[28]

The point of these examples is to remind you of the importance of swimming against the tide when it comes to investing. Just as a herd of investors can drive down a stock's price, so can they drive up a stock's price to unsustainable levels. To take advantage of market psychology, follow an optimistic trend for as long as possible, while being careful not to follow the herd off the cliff. The key is knowing when to sell your stock to take a profit. Similarly, when the crowd is pessimistic and nobody wants to buy can be a good time to dive back into the market. Of course, knowing just when to buy and sell is difficult. That's where a qualified financial planner with a proven track record can help. As I stress to clients, investing to build wealth is not magic, it's a long-term process.

Taking too Little Risk

We all know the dangers of risky investments, or at least we should. But is it possible to take too little risk? It turns out that, yes, a stress on safety can have an adverse impact on long-term savings. The sad truth is, is that a portfolio containing too little risk can leave you feeling safe but sorry as you miss out when the stock market rallies. That's because the ultra-safe investor doesn't look beyond the safety of fixed-income instruments, such as government bonds, term deposits, and money-market funds. Fixed-income investments are basically loans made by an investor to a corporate or government borrower, in exchange for which investors receive fixed-interest payments (or coupon rates) until their principal (or par value) is repaid at maturity, anywhere from a few months to thirty years. The problem is that too many fixed-rate investments put a cap on your portfolio's growth. And too little growth in your investments can leave you with a shortfall in your retirement years, not to mention unable to reach other financial goals such as your children's education or a new home.

What you need to know is that very low risk almost always results in low returns. In July 2012, for example, the yield on a ten-year US Treasury note fell to a record low of 1.411%.[29] Although interest rates are expected to rise again, bond prices will fall. So while the interest rate may be better, the investor is losing principal—that is, he or she is losing the initial investment. For example, a five-year Guaranteed Investment Certificate (GIC) is yielding around 3%. Taking into account an average marginal tax rate (the tax paid on any additional income) of 30%, and an inflation rate of 3.5%, an investor will lose -1.4% in purchasing power each year, or -7% in real terms in five years. Moreover, by investing in bonds with a long maturity date, you're taking the very real risk that inflation will rob your money of its purchasing power. Perhaps an even greater risk associated with rising interest is the missed profits from competing investments that you give up by putting your life savings in very low-risk investments.

In other words, like any investment vehicle, fixed-income instruments carry some risk. As an investor, you need to realize that risk is something to be managed, not totally avoided. Absolute safety just doesn't exist in financial markets. So keep in mind that a good portfolio is risky enough to provide returns that can at least keep up with inflation, while safe enough to protect your wealth from financial havoc. This is where it pays to be a contrarian when it comes to investing. For example, I like to advise my Canadian clients that, with so many people buying low-interest GICs from the banks, the smart thing to do is invest directly in the banks since they are the ones making a profit. Or if you own a rental property in Canada, my advice might be to sell while prices are at their peak. Take the money and invest in a short-term fixed income vehicle for two or three years and then buy again when housing prices drop. The key is to invest in a manner that differs from conventional wisdom when the consensus opinion appears to be wrong.

A Manifesto for Investing

Here are a few simple guidelines I share with clients to help them through the up-and-down swings that are part of normal market activity. I share them with you now so that you too can start taking steps to achieve your financial goals and avoid the worst mistakes investors make.

Develop a Long-Term Investment Plan and Stick with It

A long-term investment plan helps you remain focused on your goals while the market fluctuates. An investment plan specifies your investment goals and objectives and describes the strategies that will help you meet those objectives. It states what you will invest in, how you will invest, why you will invest, what percentage of your money you will invest, and so on. It also includes information about how much risk you're willing to take and, depending on your situation, may include guidelines on minimizing income and estate taxes and planning the disposition of your assets in the case of death. Drafting a strategic investment plan that is tailored to your risk tolerance gives you greater control over knee-jerk reactions. Instead of feeling anxious about potential short-term losses, you can feel confident that the returns generated will generally remain within your comfort level.

Invest Regularly

Successful investors know that it pays to invest regularly. Instead of worrying about investing at the right or wrong time, regular investing can help you to contribute the maximum each year and avoid having to anticipate market movements. Regular investing enables you to take advantage of dollar-cost averaging, investing the same amount regularly (e.g., every month or every pay period) over time in a particular investment or portfolio. By doing so, you end up buying more shares when prices are low and fewer shares when prices are high. Dollar-cost averaging effectively lowers the overall cost of shares purchased over time. It also minimizes the risk of being swept away by fear or greed and bailing out of a carefully planned investment too early or stuffing your portfolio with high-flying stocks that suddenly plunge in value.

Create a Diversified Portfolio

A diversified portfolio includes investments from different asset classes, such as stocks, bonds, and money-market securities. By constructing a portfolio with a certain percentage of cash, equity, bonds, and so on, you reduce the risks associated with a specific asset class and ensure that at least a portion of your holdings is always doing well. Diversification minimizes the volatility in your portfolio and ensures steadier returns over time. The trick is determining the best mix of assets, a daunting task given the many securities from which to choose. But a sensible asset allocation will take into account your desired rate of return, your risk tolerance, investment goals, time horizon, and available capital. Generally, however, a diversified portfolio includes a mix of domestic and, because they may respond differently to economic conditions, international stocks and bonds to offset weak performance at home.

Set Specific Goals for Yourself

When setting your financial goals, make sure they are specific and measurable. For example, "I want to retire comfortably" could become "I want to be able to spend $5,000 a year for travel after I retire at age sixty-five." Whether you want to save money for retirement, buy a yacht, or start a business, you need to allocate investment assets at a level of risk you can tolerate. Differentiating your goals by time horizon to determine when you'll need the money will also help. For example, goals are typically short term (one to three years), intermediate term (three to ten years), or long term (ten-plus years). Whatever your goals, make them tangible by setting a dollar amount to save each month and then automating the investment process. Watching your savings grow through regular investments can help keep you motivated to stick with your plan when the markets are turbulent.

Get Regular Financial Health Check-Ups

Once your investment plan is up and running, you need to carefully review your plan at least once a year to make sure you're on track to achieving your goals. Things change, and so do your priorities. Any major life event, from a job promotion or a layoff, a divorce or a new baby, to the decision to buy a new home, can have an impact on your income and how much you can save. So an annual check-up is a good time to revisit your goals and investment time horizon, and reassess your risk tolerance based on your current financial situation. It might also be a good time to look at your beneficiary choices too. Doing so allows you to determine your progress on your goals and make any necessary adjustments like rebalancing your portfolio. Rebalancing is a means for getting your investments back to your original asset allocation percentages by buying or selling assets in your portfolio. If you find that your investment strategy or risk tolerance has changed because of changes in your life, you can use rebalancing to create a new mix of asset classes in your portfolio.

Work with a Certified Financial Planner

Investment giants like Warren Buffet are few and far between. The truth is, most of us need the help of a certified financial planner when devising an investment plan to meet our long-term goals since we never got much instruction in managing our money. Certified financial planners assess every aspect of your financial life—including saving, investments, insurance, taxes, retirement, and estate planning—and help you develop a detailed plan for meeting all your financial goals. But be careful. Just about anyone can call themselves a "financial planner" or "advisor," but not all of them have the necessary education, skills, or expertise to create a customized investment strategy that will achieve your goals. Many so-called financial planners are licensed only to sell specific mutual funds, stocks, and bonds, which makes them more interested in earning their commission than making money for you. What you need is a certified financial planner; someone trained in money management, investing, tax, estate planning and insurance and who has financial planning experience. A certified financial planner is your best bet for taking advantage of financial opportunities and best practices.

Investing for the Long Haul

Investing is not magic. Growing wealth is a long-term endeavor, and the best advice is to start investing early and then to invest regularly and often. As you commit to your investment plan, you'll start to realize that achieving and maintaining financial success is a slow process with small gains in the short-term adding up to big gains over the long-term. You will learn, become more focused, and realize that investing is not about getting rich quickly but about investing in a diversified portfolio for many years.

Key Takeaways

- High levels of investor optimism are a sure danger sign of an overvalued speculative bubble that is usually followed by a stock market decline.

- Investors should make decisions based on information and analysis, not risky, speculative forecasts. Don't fall for the trap of believing that this particular time will be different.

- A long-term investment plan helps you remain focused on your goals while the market fluctuates.

- Regular investing enables you to take advantage of dollar-cost averaging, investing the same amount regularly (e.g., every month or every pay period) over time in a particular investment or portfolio.

- A diversified portfolio reduces the risk associated with a specific asset class and ensures that at least a portion of your holdings is always doing well.

- Carefully review your investment plan at least once a year to make sure you're on track to achieving your goals.

- You need a certified financial planner, someone who has undertaken training in money management, investing, tax, estate planning and insurance and who has financial planning experience.

ENDNOTES

[1] John Hussman,"Passed Pawns Hussman Funds," Advisor Perspectives, 15 October 2012. <http://www.advisorperspectives.com/commentaries/hussman_101512.php>

[2] PBS, "Timeline: A Selected Wall Street Chronology," *American Experience: The Crash of 1929*, 2009.
<http://www.pbs.org/wgbh/americanexperience/features/timeline/crash/>

[3] Fisher qtd. in "The Bright Side of Bubbles," by Edward Teach, *CFO Magazine*, 1 May 2007. <http://www.cfo.com/article.cfm/9059304/1/c_9064230>

[4] PBS, 2009.

[5] Richard Lambert, "Crashes, Bangs & Wallops," *Financial Times*, 19 July 2008. <http://www.ft.com/intl/cms/s/0/7173bb6a-552a-11dd-ae9c-000077b07658.html#axzz2AhUjMRtp>

[6] Jennifer Rosenberg, "The Stock Market Crash of 1929," About.com. <http://history1900s.about.com/od/1920s/a/stockcrash1929.htm>

[7] Robert J. Samuelson, "Why Japan Fell . . . and What It Teaches Us," *The Daily Beast*, 12 November 2010. <http://www.thedailybeast.com/newsweek/2010/11/13/samuelson-why-japan-fell-and-what-it-teaches-us.html>

[8] PBS, "Famous Bubbles: From Tulipmania to Japan's 'Bubble Economy'," *Dot Con* on *Frontline*, January 2002.
<http://www.pbs.org/wgbh/pages/frontline/shows/dotcon/historical/bubbles.html>

[9] Ibid.

[10] Samuelson, 12 November 2010.

[11] Richard Katz, *Japan—The System That Soured: The Rise and Fall of the Japanese Economic Miracle*, M. E. Sharpe, Inc. 1998.

[12] Paul Starr, "The Great Telecom Implosion," *American Prospect*, 8 September 2002. <http://www.princeton.edu/~starr/articles/articles02/Starr-TelecomImplosion-9-02.htm>

[13] Gene Callahan, "Times Are Hard: On the Causes of the Business Cycle," Ludwig von Mises Institute, 28 April 2006. <http://mises.org/daily/2121>

[14] Ibid.

[15] Ambrose Evans-Pritchard, "No Mercy Now, No Bail-Out Later," *Daily Telegraph*, 23 March 2006.

[16] Neal C. Hogan, *The End of the Third Bubble*, BDC Advisors, Winter 2009.
<http://bdcimpact.com/docs/TheThirdBubble.pdf>

[17] *Bloomberg BusinessWeek*, "Bubble, Bubble —Then Trouble," 18 December 2005.

[18] Stiff qtd. in *Bloomberg BusinessWeek*, 18 December 2005.

[19] Warren Buffet, "Buy American. I Am," *New York Times*, 16 October 2008.
<http://www.nytimes.com/2008/10/17/opinion/17buffett.html>

[20] Hobart King, "The Many Uses of Gold," Geology.com, N.d.
<http://geology.com/minerals/gold/uses-of-gold.shtml>

[21] Benjamin C. Sullivan, "Understanding Investor Biases," Palisades Hudson
Financial Group, N.d.
<http://www.palisadeshudson.com/2011/10/understanding-investor-biases/>

[22] World Gold Council, "Interactive Gold Price Chart and Downloads: From
23 October 2002 to 30 October 2012."
<http://www.gold.org/investment/statistics/gold_price_chart/>

[23] Investors Group, *Retirement Today*, Winter 2011.

[24] Bank for International Settlements, "Triennial Central Bank Survey of Foreign
Exchange and OTC Derivatives Market Activity in April 2010: Preliminary
Global Results—Turnover," 1 September 2010.
<http://www.bis.org/press/p100901.htm>

[25] Ben Fok, "Foreign Currency Investing Pitfalls," *Business Times*, 23 April
2008. <http://www.asiaone.com/Business/My%2BMoney/Starting%2BOut/
Investments%2BAnd%2BSavings/Story/A1Story20080424-61549.html>

[26] Craig Charney, "Political Will: What Is It? How Is It Measured?" Charney
Research, May 2009. <http://www.charneyresearch.com/pdf/09May5_Charney_
Newsletter_Political_Will.pdf>

[27] Expat Info Desk, "Expats Dismayed at Devaluation of Swiss Franc,"
9 September 2011. <http://www.expatinfodesk.com/news/2011/09/09/expats-
dismayed-at-devaluation-of-swiss-franc/>

[28] Jonathan Wheatley and Peter Garnham, "Brazil in 'Currency War' Alert,"
Financial Times, 27 September 2010. <http://www.ft.com/intl/cms/s/0/33ff9624-
ca48-11df-a860-00144feab49a.html#axzz2At9weKxl>

[29] 4 Traders, "Spanish Bond Yields Climb as Fears Intensify," 23 July 2012.
<http://www.4-traders.com/news/Spanish-Bond-Yields-Climb-as-Fears-
Intensify--14425279/>

Chapter Ten

HOW TO CHOOSE A FINANCIAL PLANNER AND OUTSMART YOUR BIASES

Good plans shape good decisions. That's why good planning helps to make elusive dreams come true. – Geoffrey Fisher

DOES THIS SOUND like you? You're a successful business owner who has worked hard to build your business and generate income as quickly as possible. But now you're over fifty and starting to consider retirement and exit strategies for the first time. Because you've put all your energy into building the business, you have no succession plan or any knowledge of the pros and cons of the several ways you can cash out.

How about this? You're finally setting up your family medical practice after years of residency and sacrifice, and you're looking for ways to improve your tax situation. Or this: you're a business executive with a retirement plan but still not completely sure you'll have enough money in retirement to maintain your current lifestyle and handle any unexpected expenses, such as medical costs.

If any of these scenarios sound familiar, you may need the help of a financial planner. Truth be told, most people need a planner. The range of financial products and services available to individuals today has become far more complex and, as a result, much more difficult to understand. And the wealthier and older you are, the more complex your finances become since you must deal with a host of issues, from taxes and asset protection to investments and retirement advice.

Even if you've been managing your money on your own, you could benefit from a financial planner. Two recent research studies indicate that, whatever your goals—whether it's to protect your business and your net worth, save for a home or a child's education, or protect your family in the event of death or illness—the key to a prosperous future is using a financial advisor and having a financial plan. In Canada, for example, independent research from the Montreal-based Centre for Interuniversity Research and Analysis on Organizations (CIRANO) "offers the strongest evidence to date of the link between the presence of financial advice and the accumulation of financial wealth."[1] The study, the largest in Canada, is based on Ipsos Reid surveys in 2010 and 2011from over 10,000 households. Nor are Canadians unique in finding value in professional financial advice. In the US, Putnam Investments surveyed nearly 4,000 working Americans for its 2012 lifetime income research report and found that using a financial advisor and having a financial plan are key to a secure retirement.[2]

What a Financial Planner Can Do for You

So what can you expect from a financial planner?

Financial planners provide clients with advice on how to create and grow wealth based on up-to-date and in-depth knowledge of financial markets and the latest investment opportunities. A qualified financial planner can advise on a specific financial topic—such as buying a house—or help you create a solid financial plan, track your progress, and adjust your plan in light of prevailing market conditions.

A good financial planner will educate you about the choices available to you to create a secure financial future. For example, imagine that a husband and wife finally retire from work when suddenly, and sadly, the husband dies just a year or two later. Now, most people assume that when a husband or wife passes away soon after retirement, the surviving spouse will thrive financially since he or she will benefit from the couple's joint retirement earnings. But an experienced financial planner knows that after an initial, paltry survivor payout, the government pension benefits will be significantly reduced. That, combined with the higher taxes that a single-person household pays means that the surviving spouse is looking at an unexpected drop in retirement income. A good financial planner might therefore recommend that a soon-to-retire couple take out a permanent rather than temporary life insurance policy as a solution to a problem many don't even know exists.

But the real value of a financial planner is the objective advice they can provide on the strengths and weaknesses of your financial situation, which includes your income and liabilities. Starting with where you are now, they will ask you questions about your circumstances and help you clearly define your financial goals. Rigorously trained to analyze your current financial situation, they will help determine the risk levels you're willing to commit to based on your wants, needs, and goals, and choose the most suitable investments. They can also help you keep taxes to a minimum, address your insurance needs, or help you plan for the transfer of your estate or business while protecting as much of its value as possible.

Finding a Financial Planner You Can Trust

A few years ago, a well-to-do doctor did what many others in his position do: He went to his local bank for advice on how best to protect his hard-earned money. The bank adviser recommended putting it in a rock-solid GIC. Although the return rate was low, he would be able to sleep at night knowing his money was safe. But the advisor didn't warn the doctor about the impact of taxes and inflation on his purchasing power. Since the interest rate on his GIC (or, as I like to call it, "Guaranteed Insufficient Cash") was lower than the rate of inflation, his purchasing power continued to fall every year even though the principal remained intact.

Like many people who don't have the time, knowledge, or interest to evaluate investment options, the doctor opted to do what everyone else seemed to be doing for financial advice because it was convenient. He didn't realize that bank employees, trained to sell products that benefit the bank, often at the investor's expense, usually don't have the knowledge or expertise to provide independent financial advice. This is especially the case since turnover at banks is quite high, given that wages at banks are fairly low. But, as the doctor found out, when it comes to choosing a financial planner, it pays to do your homework and shop around. Bad advice can end up costing an investor, especially older investors who have fewer years to make up the losses when a bank or investment firm makes a mistake.

Clearly, choosing a knowledgeable financial planner you can trust is crucial. But how do you choose? In Canada, there are thousands of people who call themselves a financial planner and more than 18,000 who are actually qualified as financial planners.[3] In the US, 208,400 financial planners were practicing in 2008, a number expected to rise to 271,200 by 2018 to accommodate the growing number of baby boomer retirees.[4] With so many planners to choose from, where do you start?

Here are a few simple steps you should follow to help you find the right financial planner for you:

1. **Prepare yourself:**
   A financial planner is trained to ask you questions about your financial situation and your lifestyle goals so that he or she can put together a personalized plan and create projections that show you when and how to accomplish your goals. So dig up your financial records from bank account records, income tax returns, insurance records, pension plan information, wills, and so on.

   You should also know what you want from a planner. Are you looking to achieve particular goals such as getting out of debt? Or do you just want some help with choosing your investments? To help you clarify what it is you want, start thinking about your major goals, for example, where you want to be in one year, five years, ten years, and at retirement age.

2. **Look for a financial planner:**

   Ask friends, family, colleagues, and other professionals you trust, like your accountant or lawyer, for referrals. Or contact professional organizations such as the Certified Financial Planner Board of Standards in the US or, in Canada, the Financial Planners Standards Council.

3. **Do some initial research:**

   Start by screening candidates over the phone or by visiting their website. Find out if they are taking on new clients and work with people like you.

4. **Interview prospective candidates:**

   Once you have narrowed your search to down to three potential planners, set up face-to-face meetings with each candidate at their office to get a sense of how they run their business. You're looking to gauge how comfortable you would be working with them by determining whether they listen to you and answer your questions clearly. You also want to find out exactly what service each planner offers and how much it costs.

Questions to Ask Your Potential Planner

When interviewing potential planners, there are many questions you should ask to ensure that you find someone who is the right fit for you and your goals. Here are a list of seven commonly asked questions; others may occur to you during the interview.

What Services Do You Offer?

Not all financial planners have the same expertise or offer the same products and services. A variety of qualifications, licenses, and areas of expertise affect the services they can offer. Some don't sell financial products but instead offer advice on a broad range of questions, such as whether you should pay down a mortgage or save for a child's education. Others may provide advice only in specific areas such as debt consolidation or insurance help. So ask in which areas they are knowledgeable and whether they specialize.

If you're looking for investment advice, be sure to ask whether they are able to recommend a variety of investment options, and if they do, whether they can explain their pros and cons. Too often, employees of banks, insurance companies, financial planning firms, brokerage firms, and investment management firms sell only a limited range of products on which they earn commission. This can lead to promotion of investment options that aren't the best fit for you and your needs.

Bank employees are in fact notorious for promoting GICs, term deposits, and checking accounts, often by resorting to fear tactics and almost always by charging exorbitant fees. As mentioned earlier, the interest returns on these so-called "safe" investments hardly match the rate of inflation. And insurance companies are no better. Not only do they push investment products with returns that, once you factor in management fees, might be worse than GICs and term deposits, they are also motivated by profit rather than the client's best interests when selling their products.

What Are Your Qualifications?

Just about anyone in Canada or the US can call themselves a financial advisor or a financial planner. That's because financial planning is not a regulated profession in most provinces and states; individuals aren't required to meet any minimum requirements or standards to pass themselves off as financial experts. As a consumer, you're best assurance for dealing with an experienced and qualified planner comes from asking about the qualifications that they hold. At the very least, a qualified planner should hold a Certified Financial Planner (CFP), a Personal Finance Planner (PFP) or a Registered Financial Planner (RFP) designation. Of these, the CFP designation is the most widely accepted. It is internationally recognized and tells you that the planner has put in many hours of study, has passed a rigorous national exam, has financial planning work experience, and has a commitment to meet high ethical and professional standards.

Are You Licensed as a Stockbroker, Insurance Agent, or Investment Advisor?

Financial planners can hold additional licenses, such as mutual fund dealer or insurance agent. These licenses give you an indication of what kind of product recommendations you can expect them to give you. If they sell products, you'll want to know how much they make from the products they sell or recommend. Will they, for example, get more from selling one investment over another?

Someone who sells mutual funds, stocks, or bonds must be registered with a provincial or state regulator. So if they do sell investments or provide investment advice, you should confirm that they are registered, and what kind of registration they hold. In Canada, you can do this by visiting the Canadian Securities Administrators. In the US, you can check out the financial planner's qualifications and background through the Financial Industry Regulatory Authority's online Broker Check program. Broker Check will also tell you whether they have had disciplinary problems or been in trouble with regulators or other investors.

The Canadian Securities Administrators also maintains a Disciplined Persons List, which reveals the names of all persons who have been disciplined by their provincial regulator. If the person primarily sells mutual funds, the Mutual Fund Dealers Association of Canada provides a listing of current and past disciplinary hearings.

How Are You Paid?

Financial planners make their living either by salary, commission, a flat fee, or a combination of these methods. Either way, you should know what you're getting into since someone working strictly on commission may well have different goals from someone who is working for a flat fee. The important thing is to get the planner to tell you in writing how he or she will be paid for the services to be provided.

- **Salary:** Many banks, discount brokerage firms, and other organizations pay their employees with a base salary. They usually receive higher bonuses for bringing in new clients or for selling certain products and services over other options.

- **Commission:** Most financial planners get paid a commission every time they sell a product, such as investments, insurance products, or loans, either by his or her employer or the mutual fund or insurance company. While there's nothing wrong with a commission-based payment method, it's important that the planner be clear about it. When payment is tied to commission, there's a potential for conflict of interest. The financial planner might be tempted to recommend products that produce a high commission or to trade excessively in a client's account, regardless of the client's goals, since every transaction generates a new commission.

- **Fee only:** Fee-only planners charge by the hour, annually, or by project, for example, when creating an individual financial plan. They are the least likely to have a conflict of interest since they are paid solely by their client, not a brokerage firm, mutual fund company, or insurance company. Hence, they're not pressured to sell you anything. The fee-only payment method is also the most transparent.

Who Are Your Clients?

Ideally, you want to work with a financial planner who has experience with clients like you—people whose finances and goals match your own. So ask the planner to describe their typical client. If the average income and investments per client is higher than yours, it's fair to question whether the planner will give the necessary time to your financial plans and goals. Similarly, ask how many clients they have. If they have a lot of clients, you may not get the kind of service you want or you may find yourself working with a more junior person. It's also a good idea to ask for references from clients with a similar background and goals as yours.

How Do You Work?

Not every planner works with clients in the same way. You should ask how they start with a new client, and whether they will work directly with you themselves or have others in the office assist in the process.

If you will be working with others, you may want to meet with them. Also ask how the planner will keep you informed, and how often you can expect to meet.

What Is Your Approach to Investing?

It can take a long time to find out if you're investments will help you achieve your long-term goals. So do your due diligence and ask about the financial planner's approach to investing. Do they have a guiding philosophy or do they merely sell a variety of investment or insurance products without any formal approach? What do they do for investment research? Do they keep up with economic, political, and financial events and trends occurring in all the major countries in this age of globalization? How do they choose which investments to buy? What measures do they use to evaluate risk? You're trying to find out whether the financial planner actually has a strategy, and can clearly communicate it.

Making Your Decision

The end of the interviews isn't the end of your vetting process. You still have to check their references. To get the most insight from the references, approach the reference check as systematically as you did the interviews. Ask each reference the same questions, such as how long they have worked with the planner, what types of services they receive, the quality of the service, and why they selected this planner.

Only after doing your reference check are you to review all your notes and start comparing them. Then once you've carefully analyzed your options, you're finally ready to consider your gut feelings. Remember those? They're not always reliable, but at this point you've done your homework, and with it all the left brain, System 2 slow, deliberate thinking you need. Now you can turn things over to your more intuitive, right brain System 1 type of thinking. (If you're at all confused by the System 1 and System 2 terms, read Chapter Eight again.) Ask yourself with whom can you see yourself developing a long-term relationship. Which one can you trust and which one do you think can meet your financial needs over the next five to ten years?

If this whole process sounds like a lot of work, well, it is. But remember that it's your money and your future that's at stake, not your financial planner's.

Key Takeaways

- Financial products and services have become far more complex and hard to understand.

- Older investors have fewer years to make up the losses when a bank or investment firm makes a mistake.

- Ask for referrals to financial planners from friends, family, colleagues, and other professionals you trust, like your accountant or lawyer.

- Financial planning is not a regulated profession in most provinces and states; individuals don't have to meet any minimum requirements to pass themselves off as financial experts.

- Face-to-face meetings with each prospective planner at their office is important to get a sense of how they run their business and gauge how comfortable you would be working with them.

- The CFP is not only internationally recognized but it is also the most widely accepted designation for financial planners.

ENDNOTES

[1] Advocis, "New Evidence on the Value of Financial Advice," Special Bulletin, No. 049-10/12, 2 October 2012.
<http://www.advocis.ca/regulatory-affairs/Regbulletins/sp-bull-049-oct12.pdf>

[2] Putnam Investments, "Savings Behavior Remains a Dominant Factor in Driving Secure Retirement, According to New Lifetime Income Research from Putnam Investments," 24 May 2012. <https://www.putnam.com/about-putnam/press-releases/savings-behavior-remains-a-dominant-factor-in-driving-secure-retirement.jsp>

[3] Investing For Me, "Find an Advisor," N.d.
<http://www.investingforme.com/find-an-advisor>

[4] Suzanne Barlyn, "Consumer Issues on Financial Planners Remain, Says GAO," *Wall Street Journal*, 21 January 2011. <http://online.wsj.com/article/SB10001424052748704590704576092024281308678.html>